CAREER SUCCESS REDEFINED FOR BUSINESS PROFESSIONALS

A PROVEN 7-STEP GUIDE TO CREATE YOUR PERSONAL BRAND AND BUILD A MEANINGFUL CAREER WHILE NAVIGATING A NON LINEAR PATH

THE CONSULTING CLUB PUBLICATIONS

TABLE OF CONTENTS

INTRODUCTION

It's Monday morning; you just woke up and realized that you have a little more than 30 minutes to eat, dress, and get to work. At this very moment, you begin to question why you have the job you do if you're not excited about it. The lack of excitement you experience could be for several reasons. You might find the job unfulfilling, want some change in life, or feel like you've reached a dead end when it comes to career development.

If that's the case, you're not alone in this battle. In fact, recent figures have shown that more than half of Americans want to change their careers[1]. 39% percent want a career change for a higher salary, 21% want new exposure, and 20% want professional growth. Want to know what's really shocking about this scenario? Brace yourself!

---

1.   Barry Elad, "Career Change Statistics By Age, Gender, Education, Reasons and Benefits," *Enterprise Apps Today* (blog), June 26, 2023, https://www.enterpriseappsto day.com/stats/career-change-statistics.html.

Most of us hop from one job to another when we first start out, but the average age for a person to change careers is 39. Shocking, isn't it? Think about it: if a person has decided to change their career at the age of 39, and (let's assume) they started working when they were 18 or 20, they have been in a job that was not meant for them for nearly 20 years!

This is the life that some of us lived until we discovered how to navigate non-linear success using the FOCUS framework. A lot of people might not know this, but a dynamic career path opens a wide range of opportunities promising true fulfillment. Take Gianluca Iaccarino, the director of the Institute for Computational Mathematical Engineering, for example.

He was born to a ship captain and housewife in Italy. His father told him he could do anything he wanted except work on ships, and his mother was never convinced that engineering would be the right choice for him. In his early years, things like science, technology, and engineering were never a passion for him, but his uncle, an engineer himself, was a source of inspiration. Gianluca achieved fulfillment by making robust career choices. In a recent interview[2], he said: "Many faculty members have always known that becoming a professor was their calling. I'm the opposite—the poster child for a non-linear career path."

His forward momentum toward engineering began in his third year of college. He went on to work in an Italian research center and didn't want to change careers at the time, but he was soon diagnosed with cancer.

---

2.   Leslie Hobbs, "Gianluca Iaccarino: Don't Be Afraid of the Non-Linear Career," Stanford Engineering, Stanford University, March 2, 2022, https://engineering.stanford.edu/magazine/gianluca-iaccarino-dont-be-afraid-non-linear-career-path.

After recovering from cancer, he contacted the professor he had worked with in the United States and was offered a job, but he didn't have a Ph.D. Once he completed his doctorate degree, he pursued new research directions and thought about creating simulations for engineering systems.

His life was filled with uncertainties that gave him confidence, and when it came to making career choices, Laccarino believes that "It's OK to be insecure about your choices—to start down one path and then change it. Life is dynamic and always in motion."

This short story shows that he had a lot of career changes in life, and it was important to embrace them. Changing careers is a bit tricky, and we'll tell you right off the bat that it's not the same for everyone.

Some of us feel that our careers are not fulfilling enough because they don't align with our goals, values, or purpose, which makes our lives empty. Others feel stuck in a career because they've reached a stagnated point and can't see a path forward. This can be frustrating. One of the most common reasons people don't take the necessary steps for career growth is that they fear change. These individuals are afraid to move out of their comfort zone and dive into the unknown, which keeps them stuck because they think it's more comfortable to stay in the present moment.

Some people fear change because they find networking to be a challenge they can't overcome. This can happen because they either lack the confidence or just don't know where to start. Others don't change their careers simply because they fear the learning curve and skill gap that's associated with the change.

There are so many reasons for being stuck in a career that's not fulfilling. However, there is a way you can achieve your career dreams, and it's the non-linear way. There was a time when some of us were stuck in an unfulfilling career, and seeing peers achieve success only made things worse.

We know how it feels, and the only thing we wanted at the time was a way out of the abyss we were trapped in. What we learned from this phase of our lives was that the straight and narrow path for career growth is a perspective that's long been outdated. The world is changing, and your career perspective needs to change with it.

You need a new approach, a new mindset, and a new perspective, and this is exactly what we'll share with you throughout the book using the FOCUS framework. We'll start off by talking about the advantages of a dynamic approach as we explore how the modern career landscape is changing and how you can help your career and purpose evolve with it.

But we won't stop there. We'll explain how the non-linear approach is different from the traditional one and why it really matters. Once you've developed a solid foundation, we'll transition to finding your passion. You'll learn shortcuts that can help you differentiate between passion and hobbies and how you can iden-tify your strengths. This will help you discern your true calling and determine what it is you really want to do in life.

We'll take a quick detour and dive into the world of personal branding. This might be overwhelming for most people, given the complexities of branding, but we're not "most people." Together, we will cover all the steps and dos and don'ts that will help you create a personal brand and align it with your professional identity.

Then, we'll focus on how to overcome barriers that keep people stuck in the same old, unfulfilling career. We'll learn about turning failures and setbacks into stepping stones that propel you to excellence. However, to do this, we'll need to understand how we can recognize fear and self-doubt and how we can bounce back from such realities in life.

But that isn't where we'll stop because we're here to share with you a complete blueprint for achieving a career that gives you true fulfillment. Once you've completed that, you'll be able to identify your passion and will know how you can turn it into a reality.

We can tell you that stepping out of your comfort zone and following your true calling will require some skills. But no worries because this is exactly why we wrote this book, and we'll have your back throughout the journey. In the latter half of this book, we will talk about why becoming a life-long learner is necessary, as it can help you acquire transformable skills.

Near the end of the book, we'll also cover some great things like networking, adapting to a changing world, and setting achievable goals. All these things that we've mentioned (and more that will follow) will help you use a dynamic approach to develop a career that gives you the life you desire, a life where you wake up with a smile every morning, knowing that you're fulfilling your true purpose.

This approach is the difference maker that has helped many achieve excellence. Professionals like Andrew Ng, Jack Andraka, and Reshma Saujani serve as fine examples. Andrew Ng started out as a computer science professor and later worked in the tech industry for companies like Google, but the world now knows him as the co-founder of Coursera and the founder of Deep-Learning.AI.

Jack Andraka started his career without any scientific training but now is an investor in a pancreatic cancer diagnostic tool and has won the Intel International Science and Engineering Fair. Reshma Saujani started out as a lawyer, ran for Congress, and then went on to create a non-profit organization called Girls Who Code, which is working to close the gender gap in technology.[3]

There are a lot more examples of people who made it big in life, and guess what they all have in common: they pursued diverse career paths that led them to their true purpose.

This book and the information within it can help you be one of those examples. All of us at The Consulting Club are part of a vibrant community that is dedicated to helping you uncover your true professional path. Our first book, *Start And Grow Your Own Consulting Business From Zero: A Proven 7-Step Guide To Transform Your Expertise Into Income, Attract Clients Rapidly, and Cultivate a Success-Oriented Mindset,* was a huge success, and we want to build on that by helping people develop a fulfilling career.

By the end of this book, you'll have clarity of purpose, and uncertainties will no longer govern your professional life. You'll be armed with strategies that help you exchange barriers like a fear of change with confidence and resilience. You'll have a growth mindset and an unwavering commitment to developing skills that propel you to unparalleled excellence.

---

3.   Venezia, Chris. "Redefining Success With Nonlinear Career Paths." Forbes. Last modified May 9, 2023. https://www.forbes.com/sites/forbesbusinesscouncil/2023/05/09/redefining-success-with-nonlinear-career-paths/?sh=174161393f57.

But that's not all! You'll be able to set clear career goals and develop action plans to achieve them. There's a lot to cover, so buckle up for a journey that will help you achieve all you ever wanted in your career.

FREE GIFT

At the Consulting Club we believe in empowering people to create the life they want, as a gift to you, we have partnered with our certified coach to put together a short workbook that will help you identify your passion, scan the QR below for a direct download:

Scan me!

This workbook will help you to:

- Identify your areas of genius and passions
- Find a passion that also aligns with your values
- Take the first steps to monetize your passion

If while reading the book you have any questions or want to discuss anything, we make sure to answer to all our readers, please send an email to ines@arescoaching.com

We hope you will enjoy this book!

CHAPTER ONE

THE NON-LINEAR ADVANTAGE

 "The only way to do great work is to love what you do. If you haven't found it yet, keep looking. Don't settle."

STEVE JOBS

Still have a cloudy understanding of what a dynamic career path is supposed to be? Don't worry, as this is exactly what we will cover in this chapter. If you're seeking true fulfillment in your professional life, you need to have an in-depth understanding of what it means to have a diverse career path.

For this purpose, you'll need to differentiate between a non-linear and a traditional approach to a career. Over the years, we've found that many people aren't aware of this difference, and that's what keeps them chained to a job they don't want. It's important for you to know that the traditional approach, one that states that you work hard and excel in your field with the same organization, doesn't really work in today's highly dynamic professional environment.

The main reason that the linear approach does not yield the best results is that the career landscape is rapidly changing. In this chapter, we'll describe this change, and then we'll go into detail about the differences between a traditional and non-linear approach. There's lots to cover, so let's get started.

UNDERSTANDING THE CHANGING LANDSCAPE OF CAREERS

Can you think back to a time when all you had to do for success and fulfillment in your professional life was to follow a set path after college? We can too! Some of us refer to this period as "The Glory Days." All you had to do was find a job that matched your skills, do the work, and get paid and promoted.

Nearly everyone had a roadmap of success with them and knew what they wanted to do. But the rules of the game changed not too long ago when the pandemic took everyone by surprise. COVID-19 might seem like a distant memory now, but what it did to our personal and professional lives is by no means distant at all.

The effects not only linger on but have shaped the new reality we live in. The career landscape has seen a ton of different changes triggered by things like technological advancements, changing demographics, and societal values. Let's take a deeper look at each of these factors.

Technological Advancements

It's no secret that technology is a major force that's driving changes in the workforce. The tough pill to swallow is that, nowadays, businesses can do almost anything with artificial intelligence (AI). This means that a lot of employment roles are no longer necessary.

Another technological advancement that comes with AI is automation. Today, companies can automate redundant tasks to improve their productivity. While some may say that such technologies are eating away human jobs, others argue they're creating employment opportunities for those with advanced problem-solving and critical-thinking skills.

This isn't where the influence of these technological advancements stops. Other things like cloud computing, data analysis tools, advertising software, and more have created employment opportunities that didn't exist before. All of this has caused a change in the career landscape as humans are either being replaced by technology or seeing their current jobs as a dead end.

Demographic Changes

We've often found that demographics get overlooked when people try to understand the change in the work environment. The fact of the matter is that companies today, regardless of the industry, have employees of different ages working for them. Think about it for a second: you might be a millennial leading a team of Gen Zs and reporting to someone from Gen Y.

But that's not where the demographic changes stop. You might be working with teams that are more diverse in terms of gender, culture, and ethnicity than ever before. We're not saying there's anything wrong with that. In fact, we appreciate having such a diverse team. However, such demographic diversity leads to changes and challenges.

In such a workplace environment, the ideas and perspectives of a younger generation might contradict those of the older ones. You might even experience communication gaps when collaborating with team members from different backgrounds. Not under-standing and adapting to this change can limit growth, making your job unfulfilling.

Evolving Social Values

A change in demographics also leads to a change in social values within an organization. We've often seen people who don't think of this as a big deal at first, but this perspective quickly changes when they realize that people act based on their social values.

It's important to understand that these values also govern an indi-vidual's career choices and work-life balance decisions. Many employees no longer prefer working the traditional 9 to 5 hours, and due to this, companies are now offering flexible working hours and hybrid schedules to employees.

For some of us, these changes are a dream come true. However, those of us who don't hold such social values have a difficult time adjusting to them. This can negatively affect our collaboration efforts and productivity at work, which, in turn, limits the growth opportunities we have.

These factors, along with others like them, will continue to change the career landscape. The secret to excelling in your professional life doesn't lie in avoiding the change or in finding a profession immune to it. The secret here is to embrace it.

When it comes to embracing change, there are a few things that you need to focus on. We'll cover them in depth later, so let's just stick with a quick sneak peek for now.

1. **Staying Informed:** The first thing, or some might say the most important thing, you need to do is to stay informed.

Whether it's technology or social values, you must know what factors are driving change within your organization and your career.

2. **Being Adaptable:** Once you're aware of the factors, you need to adapt to them. To do this, you need to break free from your comfort zone and be willing to try new things. You need to have an open mind—who knows what the new experiences will bring?

3. **Developing New Skills:** When you adapt to changes, the first thing you find is that you sometimes don't have the required skills. In such cases, it's important to have a growth mindset and understand that skills can be developed with some effort.

By now, you're probably aware of how the career landscape is changing. So, with that in mind, let's shift our focus toward understanding the differences between a traditional and a dynamic career approach.

THE TRADITIONAL CAREER PATH VS. THE NON-LINEAR APPROACH

When it comes to career paths, we've often found that some people are unaware of anything other than the good old corporate ladder. The only thing that's wrong with this mindset is that the corporate ladder isn't good enough for career growth and fulfillment in the modern age. Before the digital revolution, one could start working for a big company in the mailroom and excel to a C-level position (hypothetically, at least).

This is what's called the linear approach or the "climbing the ladder." Those who use this type of approach to excel in their careers join an organization at an entry-level position. Their aim is not to explore new opportunities but to focus on the ones they have. Although these people might not explore new opportunities, they can switch from one company to another when seeking career advancement.

We've seen people believe that climbing the ladder is the safest approach to advancing in one's chosen profession. To be honest, it does seem like that at first. You work hard, and you get paid and rewarded for the work you do. However, this might not be the case all the time. Those working with a linear approach might end up experiencing a drop in ranking if they ask to be transferred to a role with less stress.

These individuals might even have to settle for a lower position if they switch companies. For example, a person might be working as a marketing team lead for their company. However, if the person wants to switch jobs because they're moving to a different city, they might not have the same employment opportunities available to them.

That's not all. Some other disadvantages of the ladder approach that you must be aware of include:

1. **Limited Exposure:** You see, when you work with a linear approach aiming to secure an entry-level role and then excel within that domain, your overall understanding and familiarity with the business are limited. If you work in Marketing, you won't know what's going on in Development. If you're in Human Resources (HR), you won't know the data analysis side of things. Starting to see the full picture?

2. **Fewer Advancement Opportunities:** If you work with that linear approach, you may have one or two skills that you're really, really good at. However, the company you're working for might not have opportunities for you to excel because those roles are already filled. What's worse is that you won't be able to transition horizontally due to a limited skillset and won't be able to adapt to change.

3. **Rigid Job Roles:** Employment opportunities that come along with a linear approach are often defined in a concrete way, which leaves little to no room for flexibility. This makes it difficult for you to achieve the work-life balance and personal fulfillment you want.

The modern-day career mindset, on the other hand, is one that encourages you to be open-minded, learn new skills, and explore new opportunities. The simplest explanation of a non-linear career is that it can begin in one direction and transition into something completely different. Let's go back to the mailroom, for example.

You might start working there and use your salary to get a degree in marketing. After that, you'd join a software development company working in their sales and marketing department. You might be intrigued with application development and start learning how to code. One thing leads to another, and before you know it, you're working as an app developer.

After working as a developer for several years, you find that this no longer fulfills your purpose, and you need to give back to the community. With this goal in mind, you apply for teaching jobs so you can help others become developers, too. This is how a dynamic career path plays out.

Getting goosebumps already? Hold up! There are still a few things you need to know.

Oftentimes, changes that trigger a dynamic career path come from the discoveries you make about yourself, the way your preferences change throughout life, and unexpected opportunities that come up. So, it's kind of like a "never say never" type of thing. The dynamic career approach involves switching jobs and even industries in some cases, and profound examples aren't that hard to find.

Take a look at Sheryl Sandberg, who is now Chief Operations Officer (COO) at Facebook and a great example that you can have a brilliant career without staying on a single path. Sheryl first studied economics at Harvard and went on to work at places like the World Bank and the U.S. Treasury Department before taking a break to pursue an MBA. In her case, changing careers has contributed to a big part of her success.[1] Another great example is Simon Sinek, who you might know from his bestseller *Start With Why* and inspiring TED talks. He first studied anthropology, then worked in some ad agencies (Euro RSCG and Ogilvy & Mather), and later decided to start his own business.[2] You get the concept, right?

It's important to understand that people may find themselves on a non-linear career path for several reasons, like minimum job satisfaction, unfair compensation, limited growth, or lack of fulfillment. However, before you start walking on the non-linear career

1. Gregersen, Erik, and Tara Ramanathan. "Britannica Money." Encyclopedia Britannica | Britannica. Last modified June 13, 2024. https://www.britannica.com/money/Sheryl-Sandberg.
2. "Simon Sinek." Wikipedia, the Free Encyclopedia. Last modified June 28, 2024. https://en.wikipedia.org/wiki/Simon_Sinek.

path, you need to understand why it's important, as it will give you much-needed clarity down that road.

WHY NON-LINEAR CAREER DEVELOPMENT MATTERS?

We can tell right from the start that the benefits of a dynamic career path are endless. However, the path comes with its own set of challenges, and to overcome them, you must be willing to adapt to change and learn new skills. That said, here are some of the reasons why a non-linear career path is important.

Greater Flexibility

One of the first things that stands out about the modern-day career approach is the flexibility it has to offer. You can take career breaks or work remotely based on a flexible schedule, whatever suits you. The important thing here is that this flexibility gives you time for personal development or for other responsibilities you may have towards family and friends. This is what leads to true fulfillment.

More Creativity

The thing with a dynamic career path is that it opens up new opportunities. You can work in different industries and have varying roles. This exposes you to a broader range of points of view, allowing you to meet and work with new individuals. Interacting with these professionals and gaining new experiences broadens your perspective and ultimately improves your creative thinking and ability to solve problems.

Diverse Skill Set

It's no secret that when you work in different industries, you'll have to meet different requirements. To do the work, you'll have to learn and apply new skills. While companies benefit from you using your skills, the benefit for you would be the skills themselves. Before long, you'll have an arsenal of applicable and marketable skills that you'll be able to use for your professional development and career growth.

Adaptability During Change

Remember what we discussed about the linear approach limiting your ability to adapt? Well, the exact opposite is true here. When you work in different professions, you'll learn how to adapt to changing environments, and this will be an asset for you when a career or life change is inevitable.

Multiple Income Streams

With a linear approach, you're stuck with one source of income: your salary. To earn that salary, you have to put in so much effort that you don't have time for anything else. However, the flexibility that comes with the modern-day approach allows you to work multiple part-time or freelance jobs so you can have more than one source of income.

Personal Fulfillment

A dynamic career approach allows you to have the added flexibility and time you need to pursue your passion. Imagine a life where you work based on your schedule, and you make enough money and have enough time to work on your dreams. That's what the dynamic approach has to offer!

Now, as we close this chapter, we want you to understand that today's career landscape is rapidly changing, and to cope with it, you must be willing to learn and adapt. Climbing the corporate ladder might work, but it does have its drawbacks, as it limits your opportunities. So, it's better to make horizontal moves that help you excel to excellence!

And with that, this chapter comes to an end. We've covered quite a lot here, and in the next chapter, we'll start with the FOCUS framework and learn how to find your passion.

See you then!

CHAPTER TWO

EXPLORING YOUR INNER LANDSCAPE

 "Don't spend all of your time trying to find yourself. Spend your time creating yourself into a person that you'll be proud of."

SONYA PARKER

By now, you understand that the career landscape is rapidly changing, and to excel in such an environment, you need to be willing to learn and adapt. However, it's equally important for you to navigate that landscape.

When it comes to making a career move, either vertical or horizontal, many people just look at what they'll get out of a career move and make a decision. But this approach can lead to unfulfillment in your professional life. Think about it: What good are the money or benefits if you're not proud of what you're doing?

You might be making hundreds of thousands of dollars on Wall Street, but deep down, you really want to help people and leave the world better than you found it. With a fancy job on Wall

Street, you probably won't have time to do that. Not until you hang up the boots, at least, and this lack of the ability to do what you truly want is what leads to unfulfillment.

You see, the key to successfully navigating the career landscape is to find a fundamental cornerstone that lights the way. Some of us got overwhelmed when we first heard that this was what we had to do, and you may be feeling the same. Well, to be honest, you don't have to look far for the light.

This fundamental cornerstone is within you. It's your passion, your inner calling, your purpose, but to find it, you'll need to do some self-exploring, and that's what we're going to learn in the chapter. We'll learn how you can identify your passion and your strengths, and by the time we're done, you'll have a pretty good idea of what to do.

So, let's get to it!

FIND YOUR PASSION

"Find your passion, do what your heart says, follow your dreams." All of us have heard advice like this at some point in our lives. But do you really know what it means? Do you really know what passion is? What we've found is that many people think that they do, but they don't.

Understanding Passion

Passion, by definition, is a very strong liking or commitment to a particular activity.[1] But, let's be honest, this dictionary definition

---

1.   "Passion Definition & Meaning | Britannica Dictionary." Encyclopedia Britannica | Britannica. Accessed July 8, 2024. https://www.britannica.com/dictionary/passion.

doesn't really do us any good, so let's dig a little deeper. Following your passion results in feelings of contentment and fulfillment because you're deeply inspired by that particular activity.

However, the contentment and fulfillment you get from "following your passion" can sometimes be misleading. Not seeing the full picture? Well, these feelings, or less intense variations of them, can often come from hobbies, but passion and hobbies are drastically different things.

Mistaking hobbies for passion isn't something you want to do, and you need to know how one is different from the other. So, with that in mind, let's dive deeper into passion and get a detailed picture of what it really looks like when you've found it.

Imagine waking up one morning with an ear-to-ear smile on your face. You have breakfast, work out, get ready, and leave for work. When you get there, you are so focused and committed to what you do that you lose your sense of the world, and you outperform others. You value your work and help make the impact you want to make.

That's what it looks like!

Passion vs. Hobbies

Where passion makes you lose a sense of time, hobbies, on the other hand, are just things you do in your leisure time to relax or to have fun. These things don't really align with who you are, and you don't have the desire to pursue them long-term. Passion is something you can't live without.

Passion and hobbies might be different things, but the two can overlap. Throughout life, we have experiences that change our perceptions and ambitions. This means that hobbies can turn into passion and passion into hobbies.

This is quite tricky, and some people don't realize when a hobby turns into a passion or vice versa. However, there are four factors you can use to differentiate between the two.

1. **The Pursuit of Passion As a Profession**: One of the first ideas that differentiates a hobby from passion is your willingness to pursue it as a profession. You see, you might love your hobbies, but you'll never be committed to them to an extent where you want to turn them into a career. However, with passion, you'll actively be looking for opportunities that allow you to turn it into a profession and scale it.

2. **The Amount of Time You Spend**: You only pursue your hobbies in your free time and stop when you have to get some "work" done. Once you're done with the "busy tasks," you go back to your hobby—what you enjoy. However, with passion, you don't wait for time to pursue it. You make time for it.

3. **The Reasons You Enjoy Them**: You might enjoy both your hobbies and your passion. However, the reasons you enjoy them are different. With hobbies, it's because they're fun, and there's no pressure to get something done. But with passion, it's because the activity aligns with your core values and is fulfilling.

4. **Your Improvement**: The last factor is your improvement and growth. You see, with hobbies, you just gradually improve over time, and this happens because there's no real goal you're chasing. You're just doing it for the time

being. However, with passion, you do have a goal, and you do whatever you can to improve.

So, the next time you're pondering about hobbies vs. passion, use these four factors and analyze the activities in question. The results may come as a surprise!

The Importance of Passion

Let's look at why passion is important.

Based on the definition, passion is something that aligns with your core values, and it's something that you're truly committed to and can't live without.[2] This means that you're willing to do whatever it takes to achieve your goals, and that's exactly what is needed. Having passion is what allows you to prevail when the odds are stacked against you.

Being passionate about something means you believe in what you do. You are not just in it for the money. This is important because this is what allows you to have a positive outlook on life. It's what gives you the ability to look past challenges and harness the power that's needed to overcome them.

Another reason passion is important is that it's what keeps you up and running. Yes, believe it or not, it's that simple. Having passion means you have the ability to carry on when motivation runs out, and based on what we've seen, it does run out sooner or later. Above all, being passionate about what you do greatly improves your chances of success.

---

2. TLD Group. "Walking the Talk: Aligning Passion to Purpose." Accessed July 8, 2024.   https://blog.tldgroupinc.com/helm/walking-the-talk-aligning-passion-to-purpose.

You see, when you're passionate, you just do what you do; you're committed to learning new things and improving yourself, and we all know how important that is. Some other reasons passion is important are that it:

- Helps improve your focus
- Nurtures creative thinking and innovation
- Increases your desire for excellence, allowing you to make greater contributions
- Energizes you and the people around you
- Leads to satisfaction and fulfillment

How Can You Find Your Passion?

When it comes to finding passion, the road is different for all of us. Some just know what it is, while others have to try a few things before they find the answer. However, the important thing to remember is that finding your passion is essential for the reasons we've discussed above. That said, let's look at some things you can do to find your true passion.

Look for the Highs

As you go about daily life, you'll experience both highs and lows. The lows might be more than the highs, but they're not the topic of discussion (at least for now), so we're not going to get into that here.

The highs, on the other hand, are what you need to focus on and make note of. These moments can be your speaking at a meeting or helping a colleague, or they might come at home. Nonetheless, they can bring you one step closer to finding your passion.

Pay Attention to How You Spend Your Time

Another thing you can do to identify your passion is to notice how you spend your time. It's not a secret that we spend time and money on things we like and want to do. These things can often be a subconscious expression of our passion. See if you can identify a pattern.

But what if you don't have time for things you like or want to do? Well, you'll probably have a couple of things on your mind. Maybe one of them is your passion. Who knows? If you're constantly thinking about something, maybe it's an inner calling.

Notice What You Love to Talk About

Sometimes, we talk about something because we enjoyed the experience, found fulfillment, and want to be known for it. In fact, even if you haven't experienced a particular thing, just talking about it will give you fulfillment. That's what passion does!

So, pay attention to the conversations you have. Take note of the topics you enjoy talking about and how you feel about them. This can help you identify your passion because we like to talk about what's important to us, and there's nothing more important than passion.

Ask Those You Admire

Another great thing you can do to identify your passion is to talk to those you admire. Everyone's passionate about one thing or another, whether they know it or not. When you talk to people you admire, ask them how they found their passion or if they've found it.

If you're not aware of what your passion is and want to know, the key is to open up possibilities. The more possibilities you have, the greater your chances will be. However, one thing that you must remember when navigating the changing career landscape is that you must always play to your strengths.

IDENTIFY YOUR STRENGTHS

All of us have heard this before. However, what we've found is that not many people know how to implement this saying. It seems like human nature to play to your strengths, so what could possibly be the problem?

Well, not many people know what their strengths are. Most of the time, we think we're good at something, but we're actually not, and this is a mistake you don't want to make in your professional life.[3] Therefore, learning to figure out what your strengths are is highly important.

Once you know what you're good at, you'll be able to identify opportunities where you can excel. But that's not all. You'll also find that it's easier to learn new things within your chosen field, improve your skills, contribute more, and be of more value. We'll look at how to identify your strengths in a little while. For now, let's focus on understanding what strengths really are.

What Are Strengths?

To state it simply, strengths are skills, traits, and attributes that help you excel and succeed in whatever it is you choose to do, whether in your personal or professional life. These strengths may come from different sources, including:

---

3. TLD Group. "Walking the Talk: Aligning Passion to Purpose." Accessed July 8, 2024.   https://blog.tldgroupinc.com/helm/walking-the-talk-aligning-passion-to-purpose.

- Your personality
- What you've learned
- Things you've experienced

The important thing to understand here is that each of the three sources of strength mentioned above contributes to the decisions you make and influences your actions.

If you're someone who has a confident personality, taking risks might be one of your many strengths. If you've learned how to develop software apps for different platforms, coding in multiple languages might be a strength. If you've been in a difficult phase in life and prevailed, resilience is your strength. See how this plays out?

Strength is often divided into three categories: physical, mental, and emotional. All of us know what physical strength is, so we're not going to spend time with that. Let's look at mental and emotional strengths. Most people have these two confused and, therefore, can use neither.

Your *mental strength* is your ability to focus, stay disciplined, and turn negative perspectives into positive ones. When it comes to emotional strength, many people think it's about not feeling anything. But that's not true. *Emotional strength* is more about being connected with your feelings.

However, you still need to be able to control them and their influence on your actions, not the other way around. Identifying each of these strengths is crucial for achieving success in both your personal and professional life.

Why Is It Important to Identify Your Strengths?

No beating around the bush—if you know what you're good at, you're well off in life. Seems pretty simple, right? Well, there is a bit more to identifying your strengths. Knowing what you're good at helps you perceive yourself in a different way, and this can impact your performance.

When you know you are good at something, you're likely to make more efforts and contribute more. This, in turn, positively impacts your performance and allows you to achieve greater results. You might know what you're good at, but this information is just somewhere in your head, right?

Proactively identifying your strengths is important simply because it helps you focus more. You're able to use this to take whatever it is you're good at and improve it to a point where you're in a different league than everyone else. It can also help you identify complementary skills. Think of these skills as if they're a sidekick to your main strength like Robin is to Batman.

How Can You Identify Your Strengths?

Pinpointing your strengths can be a bit challenging. It requires you to see and analyze yourself from an outsider's perspective. So, with that in mind, let's look at how you can identify your strengths.

Productivity

First, identify when you're most productive. You perform a ton of different tasks every day. Some of them don't take any time at all, and some take longer. Chances are you're using some of your greatest strengths during tasks that don't take much time. Make a list of these activities and what characteristics were motivating you during those times.

Passion

Remember what we learned about passion? It's what you focus on, excel at, and can't live without. Find out which tasks and activities lead to such experiences. They may very well be your strengths. Pay attention to the skills you use during those activities, make note of what they are, and focus on nurturing and improving them.

Personality

Do you really know yourself? Most people think that they're aware of who they are, but in reality, this isn't always true. Take time for those self-exploration sessions you've heard of online. They'll do you more good than you think. Remember, your personality traits can be your biggest strengths.

Other People

We know that to identify our strengths, we need to see and analyze ourselves from an outsider's perspective, so why not ask outsiders? One of the best ways to find out more about your strengths is to talk to those you trust and respect. These people could be family members, friends, co-workers, or anyone else who knows you. Ask these people what they think you're good at.

Strengths Tests

Identifying your strengths by taking tests is one of the easiest things you can do. The results will tell you what your strengths are, but what's even more significant is how you interpret these results and what you do with them. It's important that you take these strengths and nurture them to achieve more. Some of these strength tests you can take include:

- **iPEC's Energy Leadership™ Index (ELI)**[4]: this is a research-backed assessment that provides insights into how you show up in various aspects of your life. The assessment measures your ability to lead yourself *and* others to take positive, productive, and sustainable action. *(if you are interested in this test you can send an email to our certified coach ines@arescoaching.com)*
- **CliftonStrengths Assessment**[5]: The CliftonStrengths Assessment is a paid test. You'll be given 177 statements and will choose the one that best describes you. Once you're done, you'll get a report showing your strengths.
- **Via Character Survey**[6]: The Via Character Survey is a scientific survey that will help you identify your character strengths. The results will help improve confidence, reduce stress, and improve performance.

---

4.   https://www.ipeccoaching.com/energy-leadership-index

5.   Gallup, Inc, "CliftonStrengths," Gallup.com, n.d., https://www.gallup.com/clifton strengths/en/252137/home.aspx.

6.   "VIA Character Strengths Survey & Character," RepoVIA Institute, n.d., https://www.viacharacter.org/.

- **Work Strengths Quiz**[7]: The Work Strengths Quiz by Gyfted is a free online test. It's aimed at helping you identify the strengths and personality traits that can help you excel in the workplace.

FINDING YOUR TRUE INNER CALLING

The final thing you need to do to complete the self-exploration journey is to find what your true inner calling is. This is often easier said than done. Think about it for a second. Do you answer with excitement and a smile on your face when someone asks you, "What do you do?" Or does that question make you resentful?

Everyone we meet defines who they are by the work they do, and if they're not satisfied with the work they do, they're not happy to talk about it. This happens because what people do isn't always their true calling, and many of us miss out on it as we climb the corporate ladder.

We've often found that people don't really know what "true calling" really means. To find this, you need to figure out what you want and what excites you, but not in the traditional way. First, you must free yourself from the influences of things like money, time, career, achievements, and so on. Think about what you would do if these things didn't exist or weren't a factor.

Embracing the question "Who am I and who am I meant to be?" can be liberating, but it's something that can't be done within the blink of an eye. Many people have gone on this journey, and those who did it right were indeed able to find true fulfillment. Your true calling is what you really want to do.

---

7. Gyfted, "Work Strengths Assessment - Free Work Strengths Test," n.d., https://www.gyfted.me/quiz-landing/work-strengths.

It's important to understand that when you try to figure out what it is you want to do, how you see yourself and the early life experiences you've had play a great role. These two things can help you discover what your true calling is, but they only work when you free your thoughts from the shackles of money, time, and all those other things.

Our position in the modern corporate and social hierarchy, money, and the assets we own do not define us, but they're deeply ingrained in our minds. They're ingrained to such an extent that we think they are our true calling. Think about it for a second— your true calling should be more than making half a million a year, right?

Being able to think free from these constraints is a challenge, and that's exactly why you need to think back to the early experiences in your life. Why? Because that was the time when you weren't exposed to all of this. At that time, what you wanted to achieve was true. Take some time and think back to what that was. You'll come away with a few things.

If you're confident about those things, then pursue them because that's the direction you need to take in life. When you know what those things are, you'll probably have a lot of expectations. However, it's important to remember that expectations don't really lead to that deep, purpose-filled meaning and fulfillment you're looking for.

That's something that will come simply from the effort alone. One of the most important things to remember is that you'll find the answer to the true calling question in a quest for self-discovery. Try these things and whatever else helps you learn more about yourself, and you'll either find your true calling or it will find you.

Finding fulfillment in life is linked to your ability to identify opportunities that you're passionate about, good at, and serve your purpose in life. Once you've found these opportunities, you'll be able to excel and achieve what you want because you'll be dedicated and will contribute more.

Recall that you can identify your passion by taking note of activities that bring you happiness and that you can't live out. For your strengths, note activities in which you're most productive, and remember to see yourself from an outsider's perspective. And your true calling is a matter of self-discovery.

Remember, your passion, strengths, and true calling are essential to you achieving fulfillment in your professional life. But that's not all. They're also important for your personal brand. Your personal brand is how you tell the world who you are. If you do that right, opportunities will come to you!

And we'll cover that in the next chapter.

CHAPTER THREE

STORYTELLING FOR PERSONAL BRANDING

 "All of us need to understand the importance of branding. We are CEOs of our own companies: Me Inc. To be in business today, our most important job is to be head marketer for the brand called You."

TOM PETERS

In the last chapter, we covered how you can explore your inner landscape. We can say with certainty that if you did all that, you have a pretty good idea of your passion, strengths, and, most importantly, your inner calling. So, now that you know all of that, it's time to communicate it to the world, and the way you do that is through your personal brand.

There was a time when personal branding used to be quite an expensive pursuit. To promote yourself and tell the world who you were, you had to buy newspaper ads or maybe get a written piece published in a relevant magazine. This meant that personal branding wasn't for everyone.

Today, things like websites and social media platforms have changed the game and made branding accessible to everyone. However, this doesn't mean that personal branding is something you'll be able to do in the blink of an eye. Creating a personal brand that resonates with your target audience requires quite a lot of work.

We've often found that people figure this out only after experiencing failure and then avoid the pursuit altogether. However, it's important for you to understand that creating an authentic and relevant personal brand is essential for your professional growth. So, without further ado, let's dive into the world of personal branding.

WHY PERSONAL BRANDING MATTERS

Personal branding can make or break the deal when it comes to professional growth and career fulfillment. Your personal brand opens the doors to good opportunities. This is especially important in non-linear careers, as your personal brand is going to be your best selling point. Start thinking about what makes you unique and special and how you can best showcase it.

Here is a scenario: You apply for a job that you believe is in line with your passion or inner purpose. Chances are the company is probably looking for an employee who is passionate and dedicated to what they do, too. When the recruiter Googles your name, your social media profiles and your online portfolio (if you have one) come up. This is your personal brand.

You might be thinking, "I haven't done any branding, so how's that even possible?" A brand (or a brand identity) is what others think about you, so even if you haven't put in the branding efforts, you still have a brand.

A personal brand is about much more than just promoting yourself online. It's about how you communicate who you are, your values, what you stand for, and what you aspire to achieve. It's your digital footprint, and it lets everyone know why you're better than your competition.

Building a personal brand can be a bit of a challenge, and you don't want to post everything about yourself online. Some of the most common personal branding mistakes people make include:

- Not mentioning their own story
- Managing the brand without a plan
- Posting and sharing content without a plan
- Not defining or understanding their target audience
- Not knowing who they are before making a personal brand
- Having personal branding goals that are difficult to measure

Now, you already know that having a personal brand is essential for your professional growth. But that's not the only reason it's important. There are many benefits to having a personal brand. Let's look at some of them in detail.

Helps You Build a Network

One of the most important benefits of having a personal brand is that it can help you build a network. Professional networks are built around who you are and what you can do for others, and that's exactly what having a personal brand allows you to amplify.

Your network can include your colleagues, business partners, headhunters, and even customers. The important thing is that the content you share is of value to these people.

Opens Up Opportunities for You

Another benefit of having a personal brand is that it opens up more opportunities. Without a personal brand, you have to reach out to recruiters and potential business partners to tell your story and what you have to offer. These efforts are great, but they limit the number of opportunities you can pursue. With a personal brand, you open yourself up to others in the industry and ensure that this information is readily available, which ultimately leads to more opportunities.

Allows You to Display Your Skills

Our skills are the most important thing recruiters or potential business partners look at when making a decision. Just writing your skills down on a resume can only do so much good. Think about it: If you're a graphic designer or web designer, you'd want others to see how good your designs are, and you can't really do that on a resume. That's where your personal brand, your website, and social media pages come in.

Helps You Build Competence

We all know that our professional competence is often measured by the knowledge we have and the results we generate. When you create a personal brand, you regularly post and share content that's relevant to your niche. This demonstrates to others that you're aware of all the latest developments within your industry and can use them, too. Doing so helps increase your perceived competence, positioning you as an authority figure.

Allows You to Add Value to Others

A personal brand not only allows you to help yourself but also allows you to help others. When you create a personal brand and share content, those who read your content can benefit from it. So you not only pave the way for yourself but also for others. This ultimately increases the level of trust others have in you online and helps you become an influential figure in your industry.

HOW TO CREATE YOUR PERSONAL BRAND

Now that you know why a personal brand is essential, let's look at how you're going to create one. When it comes to branding, there's no arguing with the reality that a great story will get the job done. We, as humans, have been drawn to stories throughout history and will probably be attracted to them in the future as well.

How is that linked to personal branding? Well, when we hear a story that resonates with us, our brain releases a chemical called oxytocin. This boosts our feelings of compassion, trust, and empathy. But that's not all. It also motivates us to work with others, and all these things are what you want your personal brand to do for you.

A personal brand is a marketing strategy you use to promote yourself and get better career-related results. However, when you promote your personal brand, make sure it tells your story in a meaningful way that resonates with your target audience so you can get that oxytocin working for you.

When you're creating your personal brand, remember that it needs to be centered around five key elements that include:

1. **Authenticity:** No one likes someone who's fake, so make sure that your brand is actually about you.
2. **Integrity:** Your brand needs to show your beliefs and what you stand for, as this can help others get an idea of what to expect.
3. **Trustworthiness:** You also need to show the work you've delivered and continue to deliver what you've promised to build trust.
4. **Uniqueness:** Your brand story should be centered around the unique experiences you've had and the ones you bring to the table.
5. **Values:** You need to amplify characteristics and traits people associate with you to give your online presence a human touch and build a meaningful connection.

Now that you have an idea of what your personal brand needs to be centered around, let's look at some of the most essential things to focus on when building a brand.

Adding Skills and Expertise

Your skills and expertise reflect who you are and what you can do. When it comes to personal branding, your skills are your greatest asset. You need to identify what they are and incorporate them into your brand. When identifying skills, you shouldn't limit yourself to technicalities and tangible results. You might be good at developing websites with fast loading speeds, but if you're good at communication and helping others, you need to mention that, too.

Showcasing Certification and Qualification

Next up on the list are the qualifications and certifications you've earned. Believe it or not, they're more valuable than you think. Both these things serve as a testament to the knowledge you have and what it is you can do, and therefore, it's essential to incorporate them into your personal brand. You need to mention all of them, even if some are not relevant to the professional opportunities that you're actively pursuing. Who knows what life has to offer?

Emphasizing Core Values and Beliefs

Your core values and beliefs are another great asset you want to incorporate into your personal brand. Most people don't give enough importance to this, but these two things help show who you are as a person and how you work as a professional. If your core values and beliefs align with the organizations you're applying to, it can improve your chances of being hired. Incorporating these two things in your personal brand will also help you humanize your online presence.

Defining Your Brand Purpose and Characteristics

The next thing that you need to focus on is the purpose and characteristics of your personal brand. When you've decided on the purpose, think of the long-term objectives you want to achieve from starting a brand. Think about the impact you want to have on others. Do you want to help others and be seen as an authority figure? Once you have the purpose figured out, use it to identify relevant characteristics and incorporate them into your brand personality through design and content.

Building Your Brand Personality

Brand personality is a set of human characteristics or traits that are attributed to a brand. It can be further divided into five dimensions, which include sincerity, competence, excitement, ruggedness, and sophistication.[1] Each of these has several human characteristics or traits within them. You need to identify which are relevant to your digital presence and audience and ensure that someone can associate them with your brand.

Selecting Key Characteristics and Traits

Identifying key characteristics and traits for your brand's personality can be a bit challenging. However, this doesn't mean it can't be done. The first thing is to determine how you want your brand to be perceived. Do you want your target audience to see you as sincere, or do you want to be perceived as sophisticated, or both? Once finalized, you need to choose the most relevant traits in each dimension and ensure that these traits are expressed through your marketing efforts.

Identifying Your Target Audience

You must figure out who your target audience is. This is a group of people who will see your brand. When identifying your target audience, create a persona and then target individuals who fit that persona. You can also divide your target audience into two groups: the decision-makers and the supporters. Reaching out to both is

---

1. Aaker, Jennifier. "Dimensions of Brand Personality." Accessed July 8, 2024. https://journals.sagepub.com/doi/10.1177/002224379703400304.

critical as it ensures you get your message across to those who are making the decision and those who are influencing it.

Adapting Your Brand to Different Environments

As you launch and run your personal brand, you'll notice the overall business environment will continue to change and evolve. Oftentimes, these changes will be highly valuable as they'll help businesses achieve better results. If you don't incorporate these changes into the overall ethos of your personal brand, it will become irrelevant simply because you won't be talking about "the next big thing." To maintain relevance, you not only need to incorporate elements of the changing environment into the brand, but you also need to talk about them.

Providing Value and Solutions

Sharing solutions that your audience can implement helps you build value and is one of the most important things you need to focus on. To do this, identify problems or concerns your target audience has. Once you've done that, figure out how such things can be addressed, and share what you've found with your audience. This will increase your perceived value, competence, and credibility, as your audience will see you as someone they can look to for solutions.

Demonstrating Your Unique Perspective and Expertise

Last but not the least is uniqueness. When you're building your personal brand, one of the most important things to focus on is how you're going to stand out from the crowd. We've seen quite a lot of people pouring money into ads to stand out, but believe it or not, the key to standing out is all about bringing your unique perspective forward. No one will follow or value your brand if you just keep recycling what everyone else is saying.

ALIGN YOUR PROFESSIONAL IDENTITY WITH YOUR BRAND

Now that you know how to create a personal brand, let's look at how you can align your professional identity with your brand. Some people see this as something that's quite challenging, but that's not necessarily the case. Not if you know what you're doing.

You see, your professional identity is the core of your personal brand, and to identify it, you can just do a SWOT (strengths, weaknesses, opportunities, and threats) analysis of yourself. To align your professional identity with your brand, you must make use of multiple media. Let's look at this in more detail.

- **Social Media Presence**: Make sure that your online presence is consistent, professional, and relevant to your brand. Share engaging content displaying your personal and professional achievements.
- **Blogging**: To align your professional identity with your brand, showcase your opinion. This is something you can do by starting your own blog or writing guest articles for others.
- **Industry Events**: Another great thing you can do is attend industry events and communicate with like-minded professionals. This will also help you build your network, but we'll get into that in a later chapter.
- **Public Speaking**: The purpose of personal branding is to position yourself as a credible and authoritative figure in

the industry and to do that, you need to participate in public speaking sessions, debates, and interviews.

- **Feedback:** Remember when we said branding is all about perception? Use that perception by focusing on acquiring feedback and using it to modify your efforts.
- **Consistency:** This is probably one of the most important things in the world of branding. You must ensure that your brand messaging and efforts across all channels are consistent. If you feel overwhelmed, pick one platform (Linkedin for example) and stick to it. If you then feel more comfortable you can expand to others like Instagram/Tiktok to have more reach.
- **Integrity and Authenticity:** When you take on personal branding, you will have to interact with your audience and other professionals. During these interactions, it's important that you be yourself and not try to win others over with a fake persona.

PERSONAL BRANDING DOS AND DON'TS

Personal branding is by no means a simple thing to do. In fact, what we've found is that it's quite easy for people to lose their way in pursuit of branding themselves; they're not consistent and relevant. Let's quickly go over some dos and don'ts of personal branding to make sure you don't have to experience this.

Dos of Personal Branding

- Do get comfortable with recording yourself. Video content is how people consume information nowadays, and you need to tap into this avenue.

- Do have an opinion about things that are relevant to you. Saying what you really think helps add a bit of uniqueness to your brand and allows you to differentiate it from competitors.
- Do remember that your online presence has limits. You can communicate with hundreds or thousands of people online, but the conversations you'll have in person are what really matter.
- Do learn to acquire and leverage references and testimonials. Publishing feedback from people you've worked with will help add an extra bit of credibility to your brand.

Don'ts of Personal Branding

- Don't think of branding as a sales pitch. The aim of your branding efforts is not to close a deal. It's to build relationships with audiences and other industry professionals.
- Don't just be active every now and then. You need to be consistent with your brand. Being inconsistent means you don't value what you do, and if you don't value it, why should someone else?
- Don't go overboard with your professional capabilities. People trust those they can relate to, and to leverage this, you need to humanize your brand by showing your personal side.
- Don't forget to engage with your audience. The purpose of your branding efforts is to build connections, and you only do that by engaging with others.

Remember, creating a personal brand is essential for you to show the world who you are as a person and what you can do as a professional. These two things will allow you to open up multiple opportunities for yourself. However, when you're creating a personal brand, also remember to:

- Be authentic
- Have integrity
- Ensure trustworthiness
- Demonstrate uniqueness
- Promote your values

Creating a successful personal brand is, without a doubt, quite a challenge. It involves identifying your target audience, developing a brand personality, and using multiple media to reach out to your audience. We've often seen that it can be overwhelming for people, which leads to fear and self-doubt.

To make sure this doesn't happen to you, we'll cover how you can overcome fear and self-doubt in the next chapter.

See you then!

CHAPTER FOUR

TURNING SETBACKS INTO STEPPING STONES

 "You can either waltz boldly onto the stage of life and live the way you know your spirit is nudging you to, or you can sit quietly by the wall, receding into the shadows of fear and self-doubt."

OPRAH WINFREY

When it comes to pursuing a non-linear career path, there will be setbacks. Some of us might not find the right options as fast as we'd like to. Others might not have the skills they need to overcome some obstacles. However, one of the biggest setbacks people face is fear.

When transitioning to a non-linear career path, many people are aware of the things they're afraid of. However, it's important to understand that to overcome fear, you need to be aware of what's causing it, too. In a dynamic career path, you must constantly adapt to new environments.

For example, since you're making career changes, understand that the concept you had of job security and stability will change. Indeed, with a dynamic career path, the trajectory is not as clear as it is with the good old corporate ladder approach. However, do not let these things scare you. Acknowledge them and understand that they can be the underlying cause of fear.

Throughout this chapter, we'll talk about the common barriers to a dynamic career path. Then, we'll focus on why embracing failure and learning from it is essential. We'll also look at how you can conquer both fear and self-doubt to break free from what's holding you back. There's lots of ground to cover, so let's get started.

COMMON BARRIERS TO NON-LINEAR CAREER DEVELOPMENT

Now, you already know that the trajectory of a dynamic career path varies from the traditional entry-level to senior-level position. With a dynamic approach, you seek exposure to different industries and job roles and work at varying levels of seniority. This nature of a dynamic career path requires that individuals face different barriers.

However, this often leads to a fear of change or failure that keeps you from achieving true fulfillment in your professional life. It's also important to know that factors like lack of clarity and financial instability contribute to fear and self-doubt. In a dynamic career path, you don't have the level of clarity you do with the linear approach.

If you were to pursue a linear approach, you'd have a map laid out in front of you. You'd know the skills and qualifications you need to have and the requirements you need to meet to advance in your career. If you were to do a good job, you would continue to get promotions or some sort of career advancement as the years go by.

However, this isn't the case with a dynamic approach. In this case, the aim is to explore different industries and jobs until one aligns with your passion or inner calling. It's important to know that such an approach creates a lack of clarity, as you don't know what to expect. In addition, moving from one job to another can create financial instability.

To seek fulfillment using a dynamic career approach, you'll likely have to work part-time jobs, take a lower salary, or do some free-lancing. So, in essence, not knowing what to do and whether you'll be able to make enough money are two contributing factors that lead to the fear of failure. Due to these factors, people often see changing careers as a major risk.

However, there are ways that you can address these factors and keep them from impacting your career choices. One of the first things to do is to change how you see failure. Instead of seeing it as something that's negative or something you can't do, view it as an opportunity. Embrace the idea that such setbacks are a part of the journey, and instead of holding you back, they serve as a way for you to identify areas of improvement.

To address the lack of clarity that comes with a dynamic career approach, create a mission statement for yourself. Think about what you hope to achieve and what fulfillment looks like for you. Then, use this mental picture as the fundamental element to make a career decision.

To address financial instability, one of the best things you can do is focus on increasing your savings and develop an emergency fund.

The end goal of this emergency fund is for your savings to last six months, even if you didn't have any income during that time.

As people implement a dynamic career path, they're likely to face some career obstacles that will feed their fear. Let's go over these obstacles now for a better understanding.

Lack of Qualifications

The first and the most frequent roadblock people run into when shifting to a dynamic career path is that they don't have the required skills or educational requirements for a particular job. This hurdle may keep you from transitioning to a different career at first; however, it can be addressed. To do this, figure out what their requirements for your desired job role are. Then, research courses you can take to improve both your knowledge and skill set.

Not Enough Experience

Another common barrier that keeps people from transitioning to a fulfilling career is not having enough experience to be seen as a competent professional. The hard truth is that you may have the knowledge and skills required for the job, but employers will want to see proof that you are able to do it. To gain some initial experience, try completing a passion project or two or opt for some freelance work. This will help you provide tangible results that demonstrate how good you really are.

Self-Doubt

Self-doubt is one of the biggest hurdles that hold people back from achieving their full potential. It's that "I know I can do it, but maybe I'm not good enough for it" feeling. Most of us who have experienced this feeling know how devastating it can be. It's like running into a wall again and again. The key to overcoming self-doubt lies in understanding why it exists in the first place. You can try to understand this on your own by doing some self-awareness work, but we highly recommend you work with a coach on this matter.

Self-doubt comes from a lack of confidence. When you think to yourself, "I'm not good enough," you're also telling yourself that someone else is better than you. This inevitably leads to you comparing yourself to others. In addition, self-doubt can come from fixating on one particular outcome. Doing this burdens you with stress and the possibility of failure.

Believe it or not, self-doubt can become a chronic state and get to a point where you're just standing in your own way. Therefore, learning how to overcome self-doubt is essential. Instead of focusing on the skills you lack, focus on what you do have and how you can use it to achieve your goals. We go into more detail about this later in the chapter.

Industry Changes

Another common barrier when pursuing a non-linear career path is the industry changes that come along with it. These changes can either come from factors such as technological advancements or from shifting from one job role to the other. However, these changes only keep you from progressing if you cannot adapt to them. So, stay updated with factors that can affect your industry and adopt a learning attitude to continue to increase your potential.

LEARNING FROM FAILURE AND BOUNCING BACK

Now that you're aware of things that could hold you back as you transition to a dynamic career approach, let's look at how you can learn from failure and use it to progress in your career.

A common perception around failure is that it means the end. Failure is not the end. Those who perceive failure in such a way tend to believe that it's definitive. However, failure is only definitive when you choose not to act. Failure does cause you to feel some negative emotions like disappointment and sadness, but you need to see failure as an indicator of another chance.

You see, when you're making efforts to achieve something, you don't really know what will work and what won't. But when you fail, what you are doing isn't working. Knowing this allows you to narrow down the options you have until you find one that leads to success.

Failure is by no means the equivalent of your not being good enough. It's just a reflection of where you currently are, and it's oftentimes a necessary stepping stone on the road to fulfillment and success. If you think about it, failure can be quite beneficial for you in the long run. It provides you with opportunities for:

- **Learning:** When you fail, you have the chance to evaluate what went wrong. This allows you to identify both your weaknesses and things you could have done differently, which creates opportunities for learning.

- **Growth:** Believe it or not, failure can help you grow as a person, and as a professional, because to overcome it, you need to learn new skills and step outside your comfort zone.
- **Building Resilience:** Learning from failure allows you to adapt to change and come back stronger than you were before, which in turn helps build and cultivate resilience.
- **Being More Determined:** Failure challenges you to get back up and push forward. This ultimately helps you be more determined in life and is exactly what's needed to be successful.

Challenges and learning curves are two characteristics of a dynamic career approach. You never really know what's coming up ahead. Many people get overwhelmed by this reality and give in to the fear of failure. However, fear is not the answer.

The key to overcoming failures lies in embracing it. You need to embrace failure and the setbacks and difficulties that come along with it. This is often easier said than done, but there are a few strategies you can use to do this. Let's go over these strategies in detail.

Embracing Difficulties for Personal and Professional Growth

Truth be told, nobody likes to have setbacks in life because they can be emotionally draining. But the worst thing about experiencing setbacks is that they cause us to second guess ourselves, what we're capable of, and the decisions we make.

Instead, view each setback as an opportunity for growth. This is one thing that will be essential throughout your journey of seeking fulfillment in your professional life. Learning from setbacks is not as challenging as many people think it is.

First, it's important to understand that failure can sometimes cause us to go into a state of denial. When people fail after putting in a lot of effort, they may refuse to admit that it was their fault, and they choose to play the blame game. To use failure or setbacks as opportunities, you must learn to take responsibility for them.

Once you take responsibility for failures or setbacks, you begin to hold yourself accountable. In doing so, you find the willingness to analyze your failures from a neutral perspective and identify factors that caused them. This is exactly what's needed to turn setbacks into opportunities for personal and professional growth. In a nutshell, figure out what went wrong and fix it.

Knowing What Guides You During Life's Uncertainties

In ancient times, people used the North Star to navigate their way, and that's exactly what you need to do. It's common to feel disoriented when you seek fulfillment using a dynamic career path. There are a ton of uncertainties involved, after all. Many people think they'll end up making the wrong decision because of these things.

However, these things are not what lead to ineffective decisions. People end up making the wrong decision when faced with uncertainties because they don't have a guiding light to pave the way for them. Make sure that doesn't happen to you; to do that, you need to find your guiding light.

The guiding light we're talking about here is your value system—the thing that's made up of your passion, beliefs, goals, and more. To identify what your value system is, ask yourself three things, and then use the answers as your guiding light. These questions are:

1. What brings me happiness and joy?
2. How can I be more connected to myself?
3. What do I want to do more of?

Developing Flexibility to Excel

The modern-day career landscape is undergoing significant changes driven by different factors, such as technological advancement and changes in demographics, as we've discussed in the previous chapter. In light of such changes, it's essential that you have the flexibility to adapt to different environments.

You can only develop and use such flexibility if you possess skills that are relevant to changing environments. Common examples of such skills include:

- Communication and collaboration
- Ability to solve problems
- Willingness to learn and adapt
- Innovative thinking

Having these skills allows you to understand the underlying dynamics of a career landscape. But that's not all. These skills will also help you think outside the box and come up with innovative solutions in real time.

Building a Support Network

We've found this to be one of the most overlooked aspects of facing failure. People think that seeking support is a sign of weakness, and they avoid it. Such an approach isn't going to do you any good when it comes to facing failure.

Seeking support or creating a network for support is not a sign of weakness. For starters, it takes real courage and strength to open up to others about your vulnerabilities and ask for advice.

A support network also allows you to connect with like-minded individuals. These individuals can be anyone, including peers, co-workers, industry experts, and mentors. What's important is that you network with these individuals and use the insights they provide for professional growth. In addition to seeking support, you should also be willing to provide it when necessary.

CONQUER FEAR AND SELF-DOUBT

We talked about both fear and self-doubt earlier in this chapter, but now, let's really dig deep into the topic. Self-doubt is something all of us have experienced from time to time, whether in our personal or professional lives. Self-doubt essentially boils down to feeling uncertain about one or more things you're capable of doing.

People often confuse self-doubt with self-criticism. However, the two terms are worlds apart. Self-criticism, to a certain extent, is necessary to accurately measure what you're capable of doing and help you stay in check with reality.

Self-doubt, on the other hand, is when you constantly undermine your own abilities; you may think others are better than you. This is what keeps you from achieving your full potential. The key to overcoming self-doubt is to understand why it exists. We've spoken a little bit about this before, but now let's dig deeper into the topic.

Imposter Syndrome and Self-Doubt

Self-doubt can often manifest due to imposter syndrome. First, let's understand what imposter syndrome is all about. It occurs when you think that others see you as a fraud or when you continue to undermine your own accomplishments.

Those who suffer from imposter syndrome seldom feel confident, regardless of how much they've achieved in life. These individuals are not able to experience happiness and wait for their self-perceived inadequacies to prevail. We've often found that those who suffer from imposter syndrome feel as if they're putting on an act.

So, why does this happen? Imposter syndrome stems from a cognitive distortion that causes people to doubt their own skills and accomplishments.[1] Such doubts can come from growing up in a family environment that was excessively critical. They can also come as a result of social pressure.

People who are part of a social circle where their worth is measured by their achievement can face difficulties in accurately assessing what they've achieved. In addition, imposter syndrome can also come when individuals feel they will be exposed or cast out for not being as good at something as they appear to be.

---

1. "Imposter Syndrome: Definition, Symptoms & Tips to Overcome It." The Most Comprehensive Coaching Platform | BetterUp. Last modified February 22, 2023. https://www.betterup.com/blog/what-is-imposter-syndrome-and-how-to-avoid-it.

It's important to understand that those who suffer from imposter syndrome undermine their own abilities and achievements on a continuous basis. This ultimately leads to them developing a sense of incompetency, which, in turn, transitions into self-doubt.

Fear of Success and Self-Doubt

The fear of success is when someone fears that when they achieve something new, they won't be able to sustain it or will suffer from it. It doesn't really have a lot to do with achieving success. That's a common misconception.

The fear is about the change or consequences that will come because of the success. People who fear success believe that it will come at the cost of something else they value in their lives.

The fear of success is not as easy to identify as you might think it is. However, this doesn't mean that it can't be done. The fear of success often shows in different ways.

- **Self-Sabotage:** This is when a person sets obstacles in their own way.
- **Self-Destructiveness:** The fear of success can also manifest as behaviors that destroy one's own competencies.
- **Quitting:** Those who fear success often quit even when the goal is in sight.
- **Procrastination:** Individuals delay starting or working on something, which can lead to the opportunity being missed altogether.

It's important to understand that those who fear success are willing to avoid activities that can help them achieve it. If this behavior continues, it can cause individuals to develop a sense of consistent questioning of their own beliefs and skills. This is what ultimately transitions into self-doubt.

Overcoming Self-Doubt

Now that you've developed an in-depth understanding of self-doubt and why it exists, let's look at how to overcome it. This is a time-consuming process and requires commitment. Some of the things you can do to get rid of self-doubt include:

Question Your Doubt

Whenever you see yourself doubting or undermining your own abilities, question your doubt. Doing so will help you stay in check with reality and will allow you to see the doubt for what it really is. Think back to the moments when you've used the same skills or similar skills to achieve your goals.

Ask for Feedback

Feedback is another great thing that can help you overcome self-doubt. Sometimes, we're just too close to ourselves to see the problem for what it really is. During these times, asking for feedback can help you gain a more balanced perspective of what you are thinking and can help you make better decisions.

Silence Negative Self-Talk

When people experience self-doubt, negative self-talk prevails. This only makes things go from bad to worse. During these times, replacing "I can't" with "I can" is helpful.

Don't Back Away from Challenges

Self-doubt can often win when our skills and abilities are put to the test and we fear failure. However, challenges and roadblocks serve as opportunities for growth and development, which can help us eliminate self-doubt.

And with that, this chapter comes to an end. If you take one idea away from it, let it be that you need to embrace failure and use it to learn and improve. In the next chapter, we will talk about how you can deal with risk and uncertainties and embody the entrepreneurial spirit.

If you think that your main blockage lies in self-doubt, we highly recommend working with a professional coach. We have seen amazing results in ourselves and in our clients who work solely on their mindset and limiting beliefs. If you would like to work with our certified coach, you can schedule a free 30 minute call by scanning the QR code below (this is a special offer for our readers).

Scan for a free coaching call!

CHAPTER FIVE

THE ENTREPRENEURIAL SPIRIT

 "[Don't] let anyone convince you that your dream, your vision to be an entrepreneur, is something that you shouldn't do. What often happens is that people who are well-meaning, who really care for us, are afraid for us and talk us out of it."

CATHY HUGHES

Many people believe that thinking like an entrepreneur is only necessary if they want to start a business. However, this isn't really the case. Thinking like an entrepreneur is essential for success when you follow a dynamic career path.

When it comes to using a dynamic career approach, you must be able to identify opportunities that help you achieve your goals. That's exactly what thinking like an entrepreneur does for you. It not only helps you identify opportunities for professional growth but also allows you to calculate the risks associated with each opportunity.

Before we dive into what this mindset is all about, it's vital to know that calculating the risk that comes with opportunities is essential. This allows you to gain more clarity about the field or industry you plan on shifting to and helps you determine what financial and skill-related vulnerabilities to expect.

In this chapter, we'll focus on developing an in-depth understanding of what an entrepreneurial mindset really is. We'll talk about how you can think like an entrepreneur and embrace risk and uncertainty. Then, we'll look at how an entrepreneur identifies opportunities and comes up with innovative ideas.

But that's not all. Once you have a firm grip on this, we'll cover how you can turn your passion project into a profitable business venture. So, with that in mind, let's get started.

THINK LIKE AN ENTREPRENEUR

Have you ever thought about what makes an entrepreneur different from everyone else? Whenever we see or hear of someone building a profitable business from the ground up, we have a gut feeling there's something different about them. Some might even think that they're special.

However, not many of us follow this trail of thought to figure out what makes an entrepreneur different. The fact of the matter is that entrepreneurs are just humans like us. What makes them different is that they have mastered the art and skill of creative thinking. But that's not all; they're also willing to grow and adapt to succeed within a changing environment.

Given this, we can say that the one thing that makes entrepreneurs different is their mindset. However, before you learn how to develop an entrepreneurial mindset, there are a few things to understand first.

For starters, many people believe that a mindset is just how we think. However, it's more than that. A mindset is about behaviors, attitudes, and thought processes. When we think, we do it in either a positive or a negative way, and this is what influences the decisions we make.[1]

Entrepreneurial Mindset, Decision-Making, and Problem Solving

A negative mindset stems from the automatic thoughts we experience.[2] These thoughts come from triggers and make us feel like we've lost control. This often leads to feelings of guilt, anxiety, and other negative emotions.

These thoughts are often irrational and are based on our past experiences, fears, or doubts that we've internalized over the years. Automatic thoughts that lead to a negative mindset can hold you back from thinking like an entrepreneur. Those who experience such thoughts often end up developing a victim mindset or a confirmation bias.

A victim mindset is when people do not take responsibility for what's going on with their lives. Confirmation bias, on the other hand, is when people see the world in a way that reinforces their own beliefs. Those with such a mindset think with prejudice and only look for evidence to justify what they already believe.

---

1. "Entrepreneurial Mindset: What is It & How to Think Like an Entrepreneur." The Most Comprehensive Coaching Platform | BetterUp. Last modified February 4, 2022. https://www.betterup.com/blog/entrepreneurship-mindset.
2. "Automatic Thoughts: How to Identify and Fix Them." The Most Comprehensive Coaching Platform | BetterUp. Last modified June 21, 2021. https://www.betterup.com/blog/automatic-thoughts.

So, in essence, a negative mindset keeps people from taking responsibility and staying in check with reality, which are not things entrepreneurs are known for. When it comes to positive thinking, some people believe that it's about having good feelings and emotions, but that's not really the case.

Positive thinking means that you're able to maintain a positive perspective when faced with setbacks and challenges. However, you still need to keep yourself in check with facts and logic. The aim here is not to force positive emotions but to have the ability to look beyond the crisis you may be experiencing.

Those with a positive mindset expect actions and behaviors to be more favorable to their desired outcome. They empower themselves with positive self-talk and can visualize the outcomes they want to achieve. Being able to think positively allows you to adapt to change and helps improve your creative thinking and problem-solving abilities.

If you want to think like an entrepreneur, you need to know that their mindset is one that heavily relies on positive and resilient thinking. This is why they're able to identify opportunities in places where others only see risks. In addition, this helps them not be afraid to speak out and share their ideas.

They're able to make difficult decisions because their positive mindset allows them to see beyond the setbacks. In addition, they're able to use their mindset to come up with creative solutions and solve problems with ease.

The Entrepreneurial Mindset Is Not Just for Starting a Business

The mindset and characteristics that define entrepreneurs are not just for those who are starting a business. Developing the mindset requires you to have the ability to think creatively, make decisions, and solve problems.

These are all things that can help you in other personal and professional areas of life. Truth be told, thinking like an entrepreneur can help you achieve fulfillment in both your professional and personal life.

You already know that using a dynamic approach to excel in the modern-day career landscape is filled with changes and uncertainties. These changes and uncertainties appear as you shift from one job role or industry to another. Oftentimes, meeting them is what's required to get the job done. However, those who don't think like entrepreneurs find it difficult to adapt to the changes that come with a dynamic career approach.

When you think like an entrepreneur, you have a positive outlook towards challenges and setbacks that come when you switch roles. This will allow you to familiarize yourself with different industries and learn different skills that you can then use to excel in the modern-day career landscape and achieve fulfillment.

Characteristics of an Entrepreneurial Mindset

When it comes to embodying the entrepreneurial spirit, familiarizing yourself with just the mindset is not enough. If you want to think like an entrepreneur, you need the characteristics that make up the entrepreneurial mindset. These are some of the integral characteristics.

- **Accountability:** One of the most important characteristics of the mindset is accountability. An entrepreneur not only takes ownership of their achievements but holds themselves responsible for their failure too. This is what helps them reflect on what went wrong and allows them to learn from their mistakes.

- **Independence:** Another great thing about entrepreneurs is that they're able to learn and progress on their own. They appreciate support from other people but don't rely on it to the extent that lack of support could keep them from moving forward.
- **Goal-Oriented Attitude:** One thing that differentiates entrepreneurs from others is that they're very goal-oriented. They prioritize their actions and know what they have to do ahead of time.
- **Willingness to Try New Things:** Entrepreneurs understand that playing it safe isn't always the best option. They're willing to try new things, fail, learn, and improve.
- **Passion:** Most entrepreneurs are often driven by their passion, which helps them stay committed to their goals.
- **Perseverance:** Entrepreneurs face tons of different obstacles and have people saying no to them many times. However, they have the perseverance to grow and progress regardless of what gets in the way.
- **Resilience:** Entrepreneurs, unlike other people, know that mistakes and failures are part of the process. However, instead of fearing them, they see them as learning opportunities to bounce back stronger.

The Importance of Having an Entrepreneurial Mindset

Based on what we've learned so far, you can see that entrepreneurs embrace both risk and uncertainty. We'll look at how you can do the same in a little while, but first, let's look at why having an entrepreneurial mindset is important. Apart from eliminating self-doubt and negative thoughts, an entrepreneurial mindset can also help you in other ways.

- **Be More Collaborative:** Working with an entrepreneurial mindset is all about being curious and exploring new things. When you ask questions, you're able to better understand how things work, which allows you to collaborate with others effectively.
- **Increase Resilience:** When you think like an entrepreneur, you know that things like challenges, setbacks, and failures don't mean the end of the road. This allows you to learn from your mistakes and bounce back, which in turn improves resilience.
- **Think of Solutions:** When you navigate the career landscape for success using the dynamic approach, there will be challenges. However, doing that while thinking like an entrepreneur will help you come up with solutions to address the challenges you face.
- **Grow as a Professional:** Remember, entrepreneurs are constantly learning new skills, and thinking like one will help you do the same. When you learn new skills, you'll be able to offer more in a professional capacity, ultimately allowing you to achieve fulfillment.

EMBRACING RISK AND UNCERTAINTY

Before we get into how you can leverage risk for growth and progress, first, let's understand what it really means in the context of entrepreneurship. When it comes to setting up a shop, professional growth, or changing careers, risk is an inherent part of the journey.

Risk is when you make a decision or take action in circumstances where the outcome is uncertain. However, it's important to understand what this means. Risk-taking is not about deciding and acting with your eyes closed. Before you take a risk, you must be able to navigate the uncertainties of the risk itself.

To do this, you must analyze the potential rewards of following through with the action and the risks that come associated with it. It's important to understand that embracing risk and managing it effectively requires three things: First, you must be able to evaluate the risk to determine why it exists. Then, you need to prioritize it based on the potential for negative impact. Once that's taken care of, you need to plan how to address it.

The aim here is not to eliminate the risk but to minimize the negative outcomes and increase positive gains. It's important to understand that being willing to take risks is essential for different reasons.

- **Seizing Opportunities:** New opportunities, whether entrepreneurship or career growth, always come with risks attached to them. However, these opportunities present us with a chance to grow and develop, which makes embracing risk essential.
- **Fostering Innovation:** Being able to innovate often requires one to take risks, as the outcome of the innovation is not completely known. However, being able to innovate is essential to stay on par with the dynamically evolving environment and the challenges it imposes.
- **Driving Growth:** Taking risks allows us to experiment with new strategies, technologies, and initiatives. Oftentimes, one of these things (or all three combined) is

what gives you the edge over others and allows you to grow.

The Pros and Cons of Taking Risks

We'll talk about how you can embrace risk and uncertainties in a little while. Before we do that, let's quickly go over some pros and cons of taking risks. Here are some key benefits of taking risks.

- **Developing New Skills:** When you take risks, you expose yourself to situations and environments you're not used to. Working in new environments allows you to nurture your ability to adapt and helps you develop new skills.
- **Achieving Fulfillment:** Believe it or not, taking a risk can help you achieve career fulfillment. Taking risks in your career means exploring new opportunities, and who knows which one might be the option you're looking for.
- **Overcoming Fear:** Another benefit of taking risks is that it allows you to overcome fear and doubt. Remember, we discussed that you need to change how you see failure to overcome it. That's what taking risks allows you to do.

Taking risks has several benefits, but it comes with some downsides, too. Although these drawbacks can be temporary, knowing what they are can help you decide whether to pursue a particular risk or not.

1. **The Possibility of Failure:** Whenever we take a risk, there's a possibility of failure. Not every risk you take will pay off. Therefore, it's essential to analyze each failure, determine the mistakes you've made, and learn from them.

2. **Financial Loss:** Some of the risks you take can require financial investments or uncertainty. If the risks don't pay off, it could put you in trouble. However, this can be avoided with careful financial planning.

3. **Emotional and Mental Stress:** Taking risks places you in unfamiliar territory. Sometimes, you may not have the required skills or knowledge needed to excel in that area, which can cause severe stress.

Taking risks does come with a downside, but they are not something that you should avoid. We've often found the benefits of taking risks outweigh the drawbacks in the long term.

Let's take the benefit of professional growth and the drawback of financial uncertainty, for example. You'll have a few things running in your head when you plan to change careers or industries. One of these things, oftentimes the most important, will be the risk of financial uncertainty. Who knows whether you're capable of earning something similar to what you already do when you're in a new industry?

A trail of thought like this can lead to a negative mindset, as it essentially is based on the fear of succumbing to a particular risk. However, if you look at the same scenario from a positive perspective, you'll see the benefit of taking the risk. Switching careers may come with financial uncertainties. However, it leads to professional growth, too.

Will you be on a tight budget for a while? Yes! However, if you take the risk, you'll put yourself in a position to learn new things. Doing so will help you grow as a person and professional. Regarding personal growth, you'll have more resilience and a better ability to persevere.

Now, in terms of your professional capacity, when you've acquired the new skills required in the new industry, you'll be able to offer more. Think about it: You'll still be capable of doing whatever you did before changing industries, plus a little something extra that comes from making the change.

You could even use your updated skill set to create opportunities for additional income and address the financial uncertainties that may have had an initial impact on your life. So, you see, a risk can indeed be quite beneficial in the long run!

Using Risk to Get You to the Next Level

By now, you probably understand that you'll need to accept risk in one way or another if you want to progress in your career and achieve fulfillment. The willingness to accept risk is the core fundamental element that's required, but it's not the only thing you need to get the job done.

If you want to ensure that the risks you take propel you further in your career, there are four key things you need to focus on. We've briefly gone over these before, but now let's cover them in detail.

1. **Conduct a risk analysis.** The very first thing you need to do is determine whether the risk is worth taking or not. However, all biases and preferences should be kept out of the analysis.

When measuring risks, focus on the drawbacks and rewards that come associated with a decision. In addition, predict your chance of success and the probability of failure.

2. Embrace calculated risks. Once you have analyzed the risks, the next thing to do is embrace them. Analyzing the risks will allow you to see what you have to gain and lose. You'll find that for a lot of risks, the benefits will outweigh the drawbacks.

However, the decision of which risks to pursue should not be made with a blindfold on. You shouldn't pursue a risk simply because it has a lot of benefits.

This decision should be made based on your values, goals, and beliefs. If taking a particular risk can help you make a lot of money but it doesn't help you reach your goals, don't pursue it. Same goes if it's not aligned with your values and beliefs.

3. Develop a risk-tolerant mindset. After you've decided which risks to pursue, you'll need to focus on developing a tolerance for them. Despite all the analysis, the risks you pursue may still come with uncertainties and the possibility of failure.

The key to developing tolerance is to remember that failure is not definitive, as we discussed in the last chapter. Instead, failure is a stepping stone or an opportunity to learn from your mistakes.

4. Seek support and mentorship. The last thing to do is seek support, guidance, and mentorship from those around and ahead of you. This will allow you to learn from their experiences and will help you effectively navigate risk.

IDENTIFYING ENTREPRENEURIAL OPPORTUNITIES AND INNOVATIONS

Now that you have an in-depth understanding of how an entrepreneur thinks and how you can embrace risk and uncertainty let's move on to the second half of the chapter. As promised, we're going to dive into how you, too, can identify opportunities like an entrepreneur.

An entrepreneurial idea and an opportunity are not the same thing. Some people confuse the two. However, it's critical to understand that an idea is just a mere thought that you have, nothing more. An opportunity, on the other hand, is a bit different.

An *opportunity* has four essential qualities that make it worth pursuing. These qualities include *durability, attractiveness, timeliness*, and *the ability to generate value* for the customers. An entrepreneur looks for these four qualities in an idea to see if it qualifies as an opportunity and is worth pursuing or not.

That said, when you're looking to identify opportunities, you need to focus on three things: solving problems, catering to a trend, and filling gaps in the market. When you're trying to identify problems, start with yourself first. See what problems you face in your daily life and which ones could be turned into business ventures.

This is exactly what Tom Stemberg did. He started Zoots, a dry cleaning company after another dry cleaning company lost his suit. But that's not all. He also started Olly shoes after he had a difficult time shopping for a pair for his kids.[3]

Once you've identified opportunities, you need to conduct market research. Focus on learning as much as you can about the market demographics, your competitors, and your target audience. When researching the market, also focus on identifying trends. These trends can be political, economic, social, or driven by technolog-

---

3. "How to Identify Entrepreneurial Opportunities." LinkedIn. Last modified April 29, 2023. https://www.linkedin.com/pulse/how-identify-entrepreneurial-opportunities-kennedy-mulenga-mba/.

ical advancements. Capitalizing on trends is another way profitable business opportunities are born.

Companies like Uber and Airbnb were founded when the entire world was experiencing an economic meltdown, and they helped people make and save some extra cash.[4] Once you've identified the market trend, focus on identifying the gaps that lie within the market and on how you can fill those gaps.

Bring existing businesses into question and ask yourself, "Could this process be done better, faster, or cheaper?" If the answer is "Yes," you have business opportunities waiting for you. Gaps in the market can also exist when there's a need that's not being fulfilled by existing businesses.

Tish Ciravolo, a Los Angeles-based bass guitar player, figured out there's no company in the market that makes guitars specifically for women. She capitalized on this gap and started her company, Daisy Rock Guitars. Monica Musonda also identified a gap in the market for locally produced noodles and started Java Foods.[5]

TURNING PASSION PROJECTS INTO PROFITABLE VENTURES

Earlier in the book, we talked about how you can identify your passion. Now, we're going to look at how you can turn that passion into a thriving business. A lot of people don't have the opportunity to do what they love for a living. The hard truth is that most people have to compromise on it.

---

4. "How to Identify Entrepreneurial Opportunities." LinkedIn. Last modified April 29, 2023. https://www.linkedin.com/pulse/how-identify-entrepreneurial-opportunities-kennedy-mulenga-mba/.

5. "How to Identify Entrepreneurial Opportunities." LinkedIn. Last modified April 29, 2023. https://www.linkedin.com/pulse/how-identify-entrepreneurial-opportunities-kennedy-mulenga-mba/.

However, if you learn how to turn your passion into a business, you'll be able to enjoy work like play and make good money while you're at it. All of us are good at what our passion is, and that's why some of us make the mistake of thinking that we'll be good at turning it into business, too.

Pursuing something as a passion and as a business are two very different things. Passion is often centered around your happiness and fulfillment, whereas business is centered around profits. This fundamental difference between the two can make it difficult for you to make feasible decisions.

Despite this, it's possible to turn your passion into a business. To do this, you need to focus on six key factors.

1. **Your Passion:** This might seem like a given, but remember what we discussed about hobbies vs. passion in chapter two. Keep that in mind and make sure that you're actually pursuing your passion, not just some part-time thing you'll grow tired of.
2. **Market Research:** To turn your passion into a thriving business, you need to have the ins and outs of the market figured out. You need to know your target audience's demographics, their pain points, and who your competitors are.
3. **Starting Small:** Businesses, regardless of whether they are rooted in passion or not, always come with an inherent risk of failure. That said, you need to keep your initial efforts small. This will not only help you minimize the risk of failure but will also allow you to gain practical exposure to running a business.
4. **Building Your Brand:** A major factor you'll need to focus on is your branding. Creating a brand identity that

resonates with your target audience will allow you to gain trust and build loyalty. It can also help you differentiate yourself from competitors.

5. **Marketing Strategies:** When you run a business, you'll need to spend some time on marketing strategies to reach your customers. This includes things like promo events, discounts, loyalty programs, and more.

6. **Social Media:** There was a time when companies could get away with not having a Facebook page, but that's no longer the case. Leveraging social media to communicate with your customers and promote your products and services is now essential, and it also helps humanize the brand.

So, embodying the entrepreneurial spirit isn't as hard as you thought it would be, right? The key takeaways here are to think positively, take calculated risks, and identify opportunities worth pursuing. In the next chapter, we'll talk about upgrading your tool kit to build a career that's truly fulfilling!

CHAPTER SIX

YOUR SKILLS TOOLKIT

 "Commit yourself to lifelong learning. The most valuable asset you'll ever have is your mind and what you put into it."

ALBERT EINSTEIN

The journey toward a fulfilling career often brings forth challenges that demand strategic navigation. In the realm of non-linear career changes, the lack of qualifications and skills emerges as a significant hurdle.

Over the past two decades, a global skills gap, economic fluctuations, and the ever-evolving job market have contributed to a 12 percent decline in youth employment[1]. In this chapter, we delve into the challenges that hinder growth as well as the crucial role of lifelong learning and skill development in overcoming these chal-

---

1. UNICEF, "Young People Unable to Access Skills Needed for Today's Job Market, New Report Says," December 10, 2021, https://www.unicef.org/press-releases/young-people-unable-access-skills-needed-todays-job-market-new-report-says.

lenges, providing you with actionable insights for non-linear success in your career.

NAVIGATING BARRIERS IN NON-LINEAR CAREER CHANGES AND DEVELOPMENT

When it comes to your career, things don't always go smoothly. Barriers may present themselves, creating obstacles that you need to navigate to successfully transition into new roles or paths. In the following sections, we'll look at four major roadblocks to non-linear career transformation and advancement. Understanding and addressing these challenges is crucial for creating a roadmap toward a fulfilling and dynamic professional future.

Lack of Qualifications

One prevalent obstacle professionals encounter is a lack of qualifications—falling short of the necessary educational or skill prerequisites for a desired role. In this scenario, individuals may find themselves in a situation where their desired career path demands specific credentials or experience they currently don't possess. This lack of qualifications requires thoughtful strategies and a proactive approach to overcome and successfully transition into the chosen field. It often involves a combination of upskilling, gaining relevant experiences, and leveraging transferable skills to bridge the gap and open doors to new opportunities.

Here's what you can do to overcome this barrier:

1. Understand the specific requirements for your target position, including educational qualifications and essential skills.
2. Explore educational opportunities, such as classes or certifications, directly linked to the role you aspire to. This targeted learning demonstrates your commitment to professional growth.
3. Showcase your acquired training prominently on your resume. This not only underscores your commitment but also positions you as an adaptable candidate willing to invest in skill development.

This showcases your dedication to expanding your skill set and adapting to the evolving demands of your chosen field. By acknowledging and actively addressing the challenge of lacking qualifications, professionals can navigate this hurdle, ensuring continuous progress toward their career goals.

Self-Doubt

A formidable obstacle to career progression is self-doubt, where a lack of confidence in one's abilities hinders forward momentum. Many professionals fixate on perceived skill deficiencies rather than acknowledging their existing strengths. This psychological challenge entails doubting one's ability, skills, and worthiness for the selected shift in employment. Self-doubt can create a mental barrier, hindering confidence and making the journey towards a new career seem extremely tough.

Here's what you can do to overcome this barrier:

1. To combat self-doubt, invest time in recognizing and appreciating your capabilities.
2. Instead of dwelling on what you lack, focus on the skills you possess. Develop a personal mantra, such as "I have many valuable skills," to reinforce self-assurance during moments of doubt.
3. Directing attention to your unique strengths empowers you to pursue your career goals.

Overcoming this hurdle requires self-reflection, recognizing strengths, and acknowledging past achievements. Building a support system and seeking encouragement from mentors or peers can also play a vital role in boosting confidence and navigating the uncertainties that often accompany a non-linear career transition.

Fear

Fear often becomes a significant roadblock, hindering professionals from actively pursuing their career goals. These fears, whether they are of changing careers or of seeking a well-deserved promotion, can hinder professional growth. When fear creeps in, it is essential to delve into its origins and understand why it exists. This introspection lays the groundwork for developing a targeted plan to manage and overcome these inhibiting emotions.

When fear clouds your career aspirations, a strategic analysis of its roots can be transformative. Take the time to pinpoint the specific reasons behind your fears. Are you hesitant about a career change due to uncertainty, or is the fear of rejection holding you back from seeking a promotion? Understanding the nuances of your fears enables you to tailor your approach for effective resolution.

Once the reasons behind your fears are identified, crafting a well-thought-out plan becomes the next crucial step. For instance, if the fear centers around seeking a promotion, counteract it by compiling a list of significant projects you've successfully completed. Document instances when you've taken on additional duties to demonstrate your abilities. This meticulous preparation serves as a powerful tool when confronting fear, offering a structured platform for discussions and pitches.

Here's what you can do to overcome this barrier:

1. Clearly define the specific fears inhibiting your career progress to tailor effective solutions.
2. Understand the fundamental causes of your worries, whether they are related to uncertainty or rejection.
3. Develop a detailed plan to manage fear, incorporating tangible steps such as compiling achievements to bolster confidence.

By acknowledging and systematically addressing fear, professionals can reclaim agency over their non-linear career trajectories, fostering a proactive and resilient mindset essential for goal achievement.

Uncertainty about Goals

Uncertainty surrounding career goals can impede professional development. Some individuals grapple with indecision, unsure about aligning their passions with suitable job opportunities or leveraging their skills effectively. To overcome this hurdle, embark on a self-discovery journey. Conduct research to learn about different careers and industries that interest you. For example, if you have bookkeeping abilities and want to work remotely, investigate organizations that hire bookkeepers for remote positions. Proactively seeking information helps you shape clear career objectives based on your skills and aspirations.

Here's what you can do to overcome this barrier:

1. Shift your focus from perceived weaknesses to your existing strengths. This positive perspective reinforces confidence and resilience.
2. Create a personal mantra that emphasizes your valuable skills. Repeat it during moments of self-doubt to bolster your confidence.
3. Engage in research to uncover potential career paths aligned with your passions and skills. This exploration lays the foundation for well-defined career goals.

By addressing self-doubt and uncertainty, professionals can cultivate emotional resilience, fostering a mindset conducive to setting and achieving clear career objectives.

REASONS TO BECOME A LIFELONG LEARNER

By now, you are familiar with the dynamic landscape of today's professional world; the key to unlocking new career opportunities lies in the commitment to lifelong learning. Lifelong learning and skill development are the catalysts for transforming careers. Below are four reasons for lifelong learning that will be a crucial part of your journey.

1. **Lifelong learning is good for you.** Investing in continuous education is not just about acquiring knowledge; it's a holistic approach to nurturing your well-being. Lifelong learning not only engages your brain and promotes mental health but also boosts self-esteem. Studies consistently show that staying intellectually active contributes to cognitive flexibility and resilience. These are the components for adapting to the twists and turns of a non-linear career path.

2. **Growth will advance your career.** The professional landscape is changing at a breakneck pace. If you're a lifelong learner, you are better equipped to ride this wave of change. Continuous skill development ensures that you stay relevant and competitive in the job market. Whether through online courses, workshops, or seminars, acquiring new knowledge positions you as an asset to any organization. Employers value individuals who demonstrate a commitment to growth and a willingness to embrace new challenges, and that's what will benefit you in the long run.

3. **You will develop practical skills.** Lifelong learning focuses on the development of practical skills in addition to theoretical knowledge. These skills are the building blocks of professional success. Whether you're looking to switch careers or climb the ladder in your current field, practical skills are the currency of the job market. Lifelong learners actively seek opportunities to apply their knowledge in real-world scenarios, creating a bridge between theory and application.

4. **Learning environments provide networking opportunities.** Networking is a cornerstone of career growth. Lifelong learners frequently find themselves in a

variety of educational environments, which provide opportunities to network with like-minded individuals and industry professionals. These networks can be used for mentorship, collaboration, and job referrals. The relationships forged through lifelong learning extend beyond the classroom, enriching both your personal and professional life.

So, lifelong learning is not just a means to an end; it is a journey that adds depth and richness to your career trajectory. The benefits extend far beyond the workplace, influencing your overall well-being and the quality of your relationships. Remember that every skill you acquire and every connection you make contributes to the construction of a robust toolkit. This toolkit serves as your guide as you navigate the ups and downs of a non-linear career, propelling you toward fulfillment and meaning.

RESOURCES FOR LIFE-LONG LEARNING

The pursuit of knowledge doesn't conclude with a degree; instead, it evolves into a lifelong journey. Albert Einstein's wisdom, emphasizing that intellectual growth should span from birth to death, resonates in the realm of continuous learning. Lifelong learning not only enhances personal development but also molds individuals into better conversationalists, leaders, and informed citizens. The dynamic nature of the business landscape requires you to constantly adapt, upskill, and broaden your knowledge base. This commitment not only makes you more versatile but also positions you as a valuable asset in a competitive market. The good thing is that, nowadays, high-quality knowledge is easily accessible and cost-effective. Let's look at some options!

Online Courses

Harnessing the power of the internet, Massive Open Online Courses (MOOCs) are a convenient and popular avenue for continual learning. Offered by universities, organizations, or subject matter experts, MOOCs cover a spectrum of topics—from business and technology to arts and humanities. Coursera, Udemy, edX, and Khan Academy provide a myriad of courses, allowing professionals to enroll for free or for an inexpensive fee. This not only helps with skill development but also keeps you up to date on industry trends. Also, we recommend you look up people who inspire you and see if they have any online support where they teach their own skills. We found that people are more likely to complete an online course if it's given by someone they admire or they identify with.

Podcasts and Audiobooks

For those inclined towards auditory learning, podcasts and audio-books offer flexible and on-the-go alternatives. Podcasts, available on platforms like Spotify and Apple Podcasts, cover a diverse array of subjects, providing insights into history, science, psychology, and more. Audiobooks, accessible on platforms like Audible and LibriVox, present recorded versions of books, enriching knowl-edge through immersive listening experiences. These resources enable professionals to incorporate learning into their hectic schedules. Personally, we love YouTube, as it offers free content on any kind of topic!

Libraries and Bookstores

Bookstores often host events and workshops and sometimes provide discounts and promotions, making knowledge acquisition economical. For business professionals navigating non-linear success, the wisdom encapsulated in books becomes invaluable, guiding them through challenges and strategic decision-making. A tip we have found very useful is to check the bibliography of any book that impacts you, as it will lead you to discover new books in the same field.

Community Centers and Local Organizations

Seeking a more interactive and social learning experience? Community centers and local organizations are vibrant hubs offering classes, workshops, and seminars. These initiatives cater to diverse interests, helping professionals acquire new skills or explore passions. From the YMCA and senior centers to museums and art galleries, these local entities foster a sense of community while promoting continuous learning.

Networking

In the digital age, online communities and networks play a pivotal role in collaborative learning. Platforms like Reddit, Quora, LinkedIn, and Medium connect individuals with shared interests, goals, or passions. Joining these virtual communities provides professionals with the opportunity to learn from others, share insights, and stay updated on industry trends.

The accessible resources outlined above cater to various learning preferences and financial constraints, allowing the commitment to continual learning to be a feasible and enriching journey.

WHAT ARE TRANSFERABLE SKILLS?

Transferable skills, also known as portable skills, are competencies learned in multiple settings that can be smoothly transferred from one employment to another. Transferable skills act as a bridge, allowing you to move confidently between roles and industries. By creatively considering how your skills apply in different contexts, you can seamlessly transition into unexpected careers. This becomes increasingly vital as the World Economic Forum anticipates that half of all employees will require reskilling by 2025, responding to the impact of job automation and technological advancements.[2]

Transferable skills are not restricted to a single job or industry, making them useful resources for people wishing to extend their horizons. Regardless of your current role, you may already possess skills highly sought after by employers in diverse industries.

Let's look at some of the examples of transferable skills.

Communication Skills

Effective communication is a cornerstone of success in any role or industry. Whether articulating ideas verbally, composing emails, or engaging in team discussions, the ability to communicate clearly is a transferable skill highly prized by employers. Phrases

---

2.   Loux, Kevin. "How to Leverage Your Current Skills to Build a New Career." Charlotte Works. Accessed July 9, 2024. https://www.charlotteworks.com/events/leveraging-your-current-skills-in-a-new-career/.

such as "able to confidently communicate at any level" and "excellent listening skills" can showcase your proficiency in this crucial area on your CV and in applications.

IT Skills

In today's technologically driven world, familiarity with common software and tools is a transferable skill that transcends specific job functions. Mentioning your proficiency in tools like Microsoft Office or experience with diagnostic testing can highlight your adaptability to various technological demands within different industries.

Flexibility

Adapting to change and navigating diverse work environments proves your flexibility. Employers value individuals who can seamlessly transition into new roles, demonstrating adaptability and openness to change. Take a moment to think about real-life situations where you have showcased flexibility, and make sure you have examples ready to bring up in any potential job discussion.

Teamwork and People Skills

Collaboration is a universal requirement across industries. Whether you've led a project team or worked harmoniously with others to achieve goals, showcasing your teamwork and people skills is essential. Phrases like "together we achieved" and "collaborated with" effectively communicate your ability to work collaboratively. A plus would be to ask former colleagues or former managers to write comments on your LinkedIn page. You can always use these as examples, and they are very powerful!

Time Management

Efficient time management is a transferable skill that resonates in any workplace. Demonstrating your reliability in meeting deadlines and efficiently planning work not only reflects your professionalism but also underscores your commitment to achieving targets. Use phrases like "planning and organization" and "excellent diary management" to emphasize this skill.

LEVERAGING YOUR TRANSFERABLE SKILLS

Embracing a career change is not synonymous with starting from scratch. Rather, it's a strategic process of identifying, developing, and leveraging transferable skills. This journey towards a new professional identity is a nuanced exploration of your strengths and accomplishments, fueled by the goal of aligning skills with new career aspirations.

Identify Your Skills

Begin the transformative journey by defining your professional identity. Who you are and what you represent to the world sets the stage for your career transition. Identify your strongest skills and assets, laying the foundation for a clear understanding of your value in the dynamic job market.

The following list offers some examples.

- **Basic Skills**: These form the foundation of professional competence. This includes the capacity to understand written instructions and effectively communicate within a team. Acknowledging and showcasing these fundamental skills is vital for a well-rounded professional identity.
- **People Skills**: Interpersonal skills are prized by hiring managers. Demonstrating proficiency in building relationships with clients, resolving conflicts, and contributing to a positive office culture is pivotal. The emphasis lies in showcasing your ability to thrive in collaborative work environments.
- **Managerial Skills**: Managerial experience extends beyond formal titles. Reflect on instances where you've overseen the work of others, trained new team members, or played a role in setting shift schedules. Identifying and highlighting these experiences broadens the scope of your managerial skills.
- **Efficient Administrative Skills**: Virtually every role involves some level of clerical expertise. Proficiency in using tools like Microsoft Office or navigating internal communication systems is a valuable transferable skill. Acknowledging these administrative capabilities adds depth to your professional toolkit.
- **Research and Planning Skills**: Transferable skills extend to effective research and planning. This includes prioritizing duties, planning company events, and navigating difficult client needs. Showcase your ability to contribute strategically to organizational goals.

- **Technological Skills:** Your technological skills are valuable transferable skills, even for seemingly routine tasks like scanning and copying documents. Embrace and highlight your proficiency in computer and technical tasks, underscoring their significance in today's digital work environment.

Showcase Your Accomplishments

Make a list of 10-15 achievements, highlighting the common themes that run across your career journey. Every interviewer is looking for an answer to the question, "Tell me about yourself." Your professional identity serves as the foundation for developing an elevator pitch—a succinct and persuasive statement about YOU that serves as a conversation starter.

Value Your Past Experiences

Refrain from downplaying your accomplishments. Instead, use your previous experiences to propel you towards your ultimate career destination. Recognize the transferability of your abilities by investigating other industries, adding "stretch skills," and strategically applying keywords on networks such as LinkedIn.

Develop a Professional Marketing Plan

Craft a professional marketing plan for your career search. Julia Harris Wexler, an advocate for informed choices, suggests getting acquainted with a new industry.[3] Identify companies in the industry that could benefit the most from your skills. Attend

---

3. "Leverage Your Experience For A Mid Career Shift." A Global Professional

conventions, join LinkedIn groups, and immerse yourself in the industry's challenges to be well-prepared.

Identify New Career Options

Take intentional steps to identify new career options. Make a list of the top 50 companies in your industry of interest. Investigate their problems and be prepared to give answers. Create your dream work description by matching your natural abilities with opportunities that provide both joy and financial fulfillment.

Emphasize the Resume as a Catalyst

Despite the changing job market, the CV remains an important tool. Create a resume that is bulleted, easy to scan, and keyword-rich. Make it a document that not only tells the story of your career journey but also generates important conversations.

Be Strategic about Your Online Presence

Distinguish your LinkedIn profile from a copy of your resume. Create a compelling headline that captures your identity while injecting the profile with important keywords. Seek recommendations from previous managers to help you improve your internet presence.

Tailor Cover Letters and Follow-ups

Women's Network | Ellevate. Last modified June 22, 2016. https://www.ellevatenetwork.com/articles/6196-leverage-your-experience-for-a-mid-career-shift.

Customize your cover letter to address the job's exact require-ments. Demonstrate how you can help the employer solve their challenges. Consider the follow-up letter as a marketing opportu-nity, grabbing the opportunity to strengthen your value proposition.

Recognizing your transferable skills is the first step; effectively articulating them is the second. As you navigate the changing terrain of your career, keep in mind that the talents you've acquired aren't limited to your current function; they're the foun-dation of a dynamic and adaptable professional future.

And with this, the chapter comes to an end. In the next chapter, we'll delve into the intricacies of crafting a strategic career roadmap that aligns with your newfound adaptability and growth mindset.

CHAPTER SEVEN

ADAPTING TO A CHANGING WORLD

 "Enjoying success requires the ability to adapt. Only by being open to change will you have a true opportunity to get the most from your talent."

NOLAN RYAN

It's no secret that the world around us is rapidly evolving, and to excel in both our personal and professional lives, we need to adapt to the change. Having the ability to adjust to the environment around us is something we're all born with.

Think about it: You have had to adjust to changing circumstances before. When you graduated from junior high to high school, then college, and on to your first "real" job, the environment and the circumstances were always changing. All of us go through these phases in life, so it's obvious that we can adapt.

What's really important to ask here is, can we harness our ability to adapt? Many people don't give this a second thought. Adaptability is a sought-after competency, and harnessing it can help you achieve fulfillment in your professional life.

Throughout this chapter, we talk about why adaptability is important, how it can benefit you, and how you can improve it. After that, we'll shift our focus to industry disruption and how you can navigate the changes within. Toward the end, we'll talk about a growth mindset and how you can develop one.

There's lots of ground to cover, so let's get started!

ADAPTABILITY AS A KEY COMPETENCY

Adaptability is one's ability to change oneself to better suit the environment. Within a professional context, it means that you should be open to ideas or changes that directly or indirectly impact what you do. Adaptability is a valued skill among employers as it shows that a person can allocate efforts where and how they're needed.

For instance, an employee who's adaptable is more capable of generating results with customer demands and technological trends, given that the two are always changing. But that's not all. Adaptability also improves your overall productivity. Those who have the ability to change don't stress out when faced with challenges.

This means that they're able to see challenges with a positive outlook and can achieve better results. In addition, being adaptable also allows you to show that you're a resourceful professional who can analyze the situation and that you're capable of leading others.

When it comes to being adaptable in the workplace, the benefits are endless. Here are some of the benefits:

1. **Become a more valuable employee.** Changes are inevitable, regardless of the industry you're in. Given this reality, employers often look for professionals who have the ability to adapt to change. This shows an employer that you can address challenges with ease, which, in turn, makes you more valuable.

2. **Develop leadership qualities.** Adaptability requires you to have focus, motivation, and an open-minded outlook. All of these are essential leadership qualities, too. But that's not all. Having the ability to adapt to changing circumstances also makes you a source of inspiration for others.

3. **Change careers more easily.** As you seek fulfillment in your professional life, you'll need to shift from one job to another. With that shift will come changes in what you do, the industry, and how you work. Having the ability to adapt will ensure that you're equipped with the right mindset and capabilities needed to switch careers effectively.

4. **Experience more happiness.** Changes in our professional lives can make the best of us break a sweat. However, when you're adaptable, you're able to pivot as needed. This means that changing circumstances don't make you stressed, which in turn allows you to live more happily.

Now that you know why adaptability is essential and what the benefits are, let's look at how you can improve your adaptability.

Break Free from Your Comfort Zone

Changes happen when you expose yourself to new environments, and to do that, you have to come out of your comfort zone. Most people find this challenging to do. To effectively break free from your comfort zone, familiarize yourself with the challenges you're likely to face and maintain a positive outlook.

Be a Better Listener

Another great thing you can do to be more adaptable is to become a better listener. When you actively listen to what others around you have to say, you can gain valuable insights. You can then use these insights to better understand the changes likely to take place, and you will be better equipped to handle them.

Always Ask Questions

In addition to active listening, you also need to ask questions. Asking your co-worker or mentor questions will allow you to gain a more contextual understanding of your industry and the anticipated changes that may occur. It also helps you learn how those ahead of you become adaptable and how you can do the same.

Don't Shy Away from Making Mistakes

Mistakes can serve as a setback for most of us and oftentimes do. However, if you want to become more adaptable, you must learn to embrace your mistakes. As we discussed in a previous chapter, when you embrace your mistakes, you see them as learning opportunities, and you will change your perspective toward them, which will make you more adaptable.

Be More Emotionally Intelligent

When faced with uncertainty, many of us allow our emotions to get the best of us. But if we want to become more adaptable, we need to be in control of our emotions, not the other way around. When we have our emotions under control, we're able to tailor our responses and behavior better, which ultimately makes us more adaptable.

Create Balance in Your Life

One of the most important things required to be more adaptable is balance. When you have both your personal and professional lives in control, you're better equipped to think with a clear head. This allows you to assess each change based on its actual metric and act accordingly.

Observe and Learn

A key thing you need to remember when going through change is that you're not alone. If you look around, you'll find a family member, friend, or co-worker who is probably going through something similar. You can observe how these individuals react to and embrace change and learn from what they're doing.

Have a Positive Outlook

Some of us resent change simply because it comes with challenges that require us to do things we've never done before. This could be learning a new skill, talking to people we don't know, or something else entirely. Whatever the case may be, it's important to see the challenges as stepping stones and have an optimistic outlook.

WHAT IS INDUSTRY DISRUPTION?

Now that you're aware of what adaptability is and how you can be more adaptable let's shift our focus to industry disruption. Industry disruption is when the rules of competition in a particular industry change because things are being done differently.

Such disruptive change happens due to different factors like competition, technological advancements, economic changes, and so on. The changes, regardless of why they occur, will impact how you do your job. In fact, the impact of such changes extends beyond just one individual.

Disruptions can lead to new products, services, or markets being developed and even displace established players in the industry. Remember what happened when the pandemic hit? Those who were at the top of the corporate food chain did not all stay there, and many of us don't work the same way we did before.

Remote work, which was not even in the back of anyone's mind before 2020, is either a perk that companies offer or a requirement that job candidates actively look for. Professionals in different industries worldwide initially struggled to work remotely, and things like communication and collaboration were challenging.

NAVIGATING INDUSTRY CHANGES AND DISRUPTIONS

Before learning how you can navigate disruptive changes, you must be able to recognize them. Changes and disruptions that require you to be adaptable can often be recognized based on their characteristics, which differentiate them from other types of change.

- **Inferior Beginnings**: Changes that disrupt industries are initially inferior to established products or services but experience rapid growth and popularity.
- **Unpredictability**: These changes are unexpected and difficult to predict, given that they are triggered by varying factors like technological developments and global events, and they happen quickly.
- **New Offerings**: Changes that require you to be more adaptable often lead to the creation of new products, services, or markets, given that they cater to demands that were previously unknown or didn't exist.
- **Impact on Society**: Disruptive changes don't just impact the industry or professionals within that industry. These changes have the potential to impact how other people live and interact with each other, too.

When you're in an industry that's experiencing disruption, your only option is to adapt. However, to adapt to such changes, you must effectively navigate them. When navigating such disruptions, it's important to understand what caused the change. We named a few factors earlier on. Let's get into more details about them now.

- **Technological Advancement**: Advances in technology can often cause disruptive changes in an industry, given that such development leads to reduced cost and improved operational efficiency and productivity. One of the best examples from the last few years has been the development of AI.
- **Customer Behavior**: Businesses, regardless of their industry, always strive to cater to customer demands. This means that if customer preferences change, it's going to lead to a change in business practices that ultimately will

lead to disruption in the industry. For example, when people started using their smartphones more than their laptops, companies had to switch their focus and improve the customer experience on a small screen.

- **Legal Changes:** Businesses have to comply with amendments to or the addition of legal regulations, which can also lead to industry disruptions. For example, when Thailand fully legalized marijuana in 2022, a lot of businesses started adapting to be able to profit from this new law.

- **Global Events:** Global events like pandemics or geo-political crises have an impact on society. They reshape customer preferences and trigger new needs. When combined, these factors dictate the need for a change in business practices.

Having the ability to adapt allows you to tailor your responses and actions based on the prevailing change so you can navigate disruptions effectively. However, that's not the only thing you can use to your advantage. Some of the best ways to navigate change and distribution include:

Staying Informed

The very first thing to do to navigate changes within an industry is to stay updated with all the latest developments. This development could be technological, political, social, or economic. These types of developments possess the potential to cause disruptive change within an industry.

Staying up to date with such factors will ensure that you're learning on a continuous basis, which improves both your awareness and your ability to adapt. To stay updated, attend seminars, conferences, or workshops. Alternatively, there are free resources online (podcasts, YouTube channels, etc.) that are usually up-to-date and have the latest news. We especially like this option, as it allows you to get to know creators in your field and be inspired by them.

Assessing the Impact

Once you're aware of all that's going on in your industry, assess the impact these changes will have. To assess the impact of a particular change, check to see how it will change existing products or services. Then, use those predicted changes to determine what skills will be required or how you could adapt an existing offer.

You can also do some online research to gain a more accurate perception of the disruptive change. If you have noticed a change in your industry, the customers have too. So, go online and see what people are saying about it. Do they like it, or do they want something more?

Exploring Different Responses

This step to navigating change is closely tied to its predecessor. When you're assessing the impact, it's important to plan how to respond to the change. However, responses can't just be based on what you feel or think is the right thing to do. The response should be based on the insight you gained in the previous step. You should also come up with multiple responses to the change, which should address different aspects of the disruption or change for them to be feasible.

Defining the Objectives and Goals

Before you begin to implement what you think would be the ideal response to a particular change, define your objective and goal. To do this, think about what you're trying to achieve by responding in a particular way. Remember that these goals and objectives can't be vague.

When you note what you want to achieve, make sure it's specific, but that's not all. Make sure it's something that you can do with the resources at your disposal. Also, come up with metrics you can use to measure and track progress.

For example, at some point, one of our collaborators at The Consulting Club saw that there was a rising demand for online courses. People do not always have the time anymore to commute somewhere in their city to learn a new skill (if that skill can be learned online). Also, by learning online, customers have more options. Our collaborator moved all her offerings online and created a funnel for online customers. It took some time to build, but ultimately, it paid off. Once her offerings were online, she would only offer limited spots for any kind of in-person workshops, and she could double her prices while generating most of her income online.

Executing, Monitoring, Improving

Once you've finalized a response and have defined goals and objectives, it's time to execute it. Constantly monitor your progress as you move forward with the execution. To do this, compare your progress with the metrics you defined in the previous step.

You must have a positive outlook even if your progress is not at par with the metrics. Doing so will make the comparison between actual and expected performance more constructive. This will help you gain valuable insight that you can then use to make improvements to your overall behavior and actions.

In essence, industry disruption can be caused by different factors, such as technological or economic changes. However, it's only seen as a disruptive change when it leads to new products, services, or markets being developed.

Such change impacts how you work in a particular industry, and navigating such changes is essential. We've discussed a few ways that you can navigate these changes.

However, the fundamental component that leads to effective navigation is a growth mindset. Let's look at that in more detail.

WHAT IS A GROWTH MINDSET?

It's no secret that the way we think about ourselves and what we're capable of doing impacts our performance in both our personal and professional lives. Despite this, some people look at challenges and believe that they don't have what it takes to overcome them. This belief keeps them from doing so.

This is where a growth mindset can make all the difference in the world. Having a growth mindset means that you believe that qualities like skills and intelligence can be developed over time. A growth mindset welcomes the idea of learning and resilience.

Those with such a mindset believe that they can expand and improve their capabilities with dedicated time and effort, allowing them to overcome challenges with ease. Its counterpart, the fixed mindset, dictates that people are born with a certain set of immutable skills, qualities, talents, and levels of intelligence. Where the growth mindset emphasizes the importance of learning, the fixed mindset states that abilities are static and cannot be changed. There are some key differences between a growth mindset and a fixed one.

- **Challenges:** Those with a growth mindset embrace challenges and see them as an opportunity to learn. People with a fixed mindset avoid challenges due to a fear of change or failure.
- **Feedback:** People who have a growth mindset see continuous learning opportunities and look for constructive feedback. However, those with a fixed mindset take feedback personally and resort to the blame game.
- **Resilience:** This is another thing that differentiates the two. With a growth mindset, people see challenges and setbacks as learning opportunities. However, those with a fixed mindset give up when faced with similar circumstances.
- **Development:** Those with a growth mindset believe in nurturing their intelligence and abilities. Those with a fixed mindset believe in natural talent and think that skills are something one cannot improve.

Both the growth and the fixed mindset approaches can be evident in life at different times. Let's say that you've just started working as a software developer. At your new job, you've been tasked to develop a program that can analyze employee performance.

This new software you're developing also has to provide insightful recommendations that can be used to improve both performance and productivity. However, the catch is that you've never done something like this before.

If you're someone with a fixed mindset, you would probably have thoughts similar to "I hope this will be easy for me." However, with a growth mindset, you would think, "I haven't done this before, but it will be very interesting."

With the fixed mindset thought, you're approaching the tasks with a negative perspective triggered by a lack of competence. Here, you hope the task will be easy because you might have what it takes and cannot improve what you have.

However, with a growth mindset, your perspective is positive. You want the task to be interesting because you know that even if it's difficult, it has something to teach you. Let's take this example one step further.

You develop the program and submit it to your supervisor for approval, who finds it's not up to the mark. If you're someone with a fixed mindset, you would immediately think, "It's not my fault. I didn't have the right tools; this idea was never going to be useful anyway." Here, you would be pointing fingers and playing the blame game instead of acknowledging a lack of competence and working on your skills.

Let's say that you were given the same feedback, but you had a growth mindset. In that case, you would think, "Okay, I have three things I need to improve; let's figure out how I can do that." With such a mindset, you're acknowledging that you might not be good enough right now, but you have what it takes to improve and overcome. Having a growth mindset is highly beneficial since it:

- Makes you more resilient
- Helps make you more humble
- Allows you to be better equipped for entering new industries
- Empowers you to deal with change and makes you more adaptable
- Enables you to work on yourself and grow as a person and as a professional

Also, let's not forget that you are not failing unless you quit. Any kind of setback or feedback will only make you better in the long run, making you more skillful and resourceful!

HOW TO DEVELOP A GROWTH MINDSET

Having a growth mindset not only improves your professional capabilities but also makes you more adaptable to change. With such an approach, you understand that changing circumstances are a challenge.

However, you also know that you have what it takes to figure out what skills are needed to tackle the challenge. You know that you can learn and acquire those skills and overcome unexpected changes and setbacks. Through the years, from our own experience, we have collected a few steps that can help you develop a growth mindset:

1. Start by identifying what your mindset is. To do this, examine your current approach to challenges and setbacks.
2. Figure out when you fall into the fixed mindset traps and identify areas of improvement.

3. Overcome your fear of failure by observing and examining how others have prevailed against the odds.

4. Seek continuous feedback so that you can learn and improve your intelligence and skills.

5. Identify your weaknesses and embrace challenges so that you can develop persistence.

6. Develop a habit of making mistakes and learning from them, and focus on developing new skills every now and then.

7. Set realistic goals that you can achieve by working with your current resources, and surround yourself with growth-minded people for constant motivation.

8. Celebrate small wins, as they allow you to acknowledge all you've achieved, improved, and overcome.

And with that, another chapter comes to an end. If there's one thing to take away from this, it is that change in industries is inevitable. However, it's something that you can overcome by being more adaptable and even use in your favor!

To increase your adaptability, you must be willing to fail, learn, and have a growth mindset. Doing so will help you see setbacks as opportunities for professional growth and improvement, which will help you harness change for the better. In the next chapter, we'll focus on successful networking strategies that can help you achieve career fulfillment.

CHAPTER EIGHT

NETWORKING STRATEGIES FOR SUCCESS

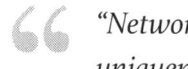 *"Networking is marketing. Marketing yourself, your uniqueness, what you stand for."*

CHRISTINE COMAFORD-LYNCH

The quote you've just read is what networking is all about. However, networking with others for professional success is a bit different than what many people think it is. Some people often shy away from networking because they associate it with awkwardness and see it as something cheesy.

But that's not all. Networking, over time, has developed a bad reputation. It's often perceived as begging for favors, making unnecessary small talk, or being opportunistic in nature. However, networking is an essential part of the career journey regardless of what industry you're in.

Networking allows you to have long-term relationships with others and helps build a professional and competent reputation.

The underlying idea behind networking is that you must meet and get to know people you can assist and benefit from.

In this chapter, we'll discuss, in detail, why networking is important and how you build a diverse and supportive network. Then, we'll cover some effective strategies that will come in handy.

Let's dive in!

WHY NETWORKING MATTERS

Most of us have heard of networking, but not all of us understand just how important it is. A professional network is essential in all stages of our career, whether we're just starting out or at an executive-level position. Before we explore why professional networking is essential, let's take some time to understand what it's all about.

Professional networking is about building long-term relations with others in the same industry and in related industries. When building such relationships, remember that the aim is for the relationships to be beneficial to both you and those in your network.

The way this works is that you reach out to those in your network, ask them for favors, and help them in return. You can build professional networks at events, conferences, expos, and so on. We'll cover more about this in detail in a while. For now, know that the more you network, the more connections you have.

This means that you have a greater number of people to rely on when you need a favor or two. This is very important and allows you to excel in your career and achieve your professional goals. We have found some key reasons through our careers why networking is important.

Build Professional Relationships

Professional relationships are one of the most important reasons for building a network. There is a common misconception that it's all about taking, but networking is about sharing.

When you frequently engage with your connections and assist them when needed, you're able to strengthen your relationship with them. Doing so not only increases your perceived value but also allows you to call on them for help or assistance when you need it.

Open Doors to New Opportunities

When you connect with others, it's likely that they will have access to opportunities you are not aware of. These opportunities could be for anything—a new job, a business, personal growth, you name it.

Actively engaging with your connections is essential. Do this, and when they have an opportunity, you'll be the first person they think of. This can help you get introductions to people higher on the corporate ladder or even job referrals.

Exchange Ideas and Best Practices

Believe it or not, networking is a great way to learn about all the latest developments and best practices in an industry. When you're connected to people from different sides of your industry, you're able to access new and valuable information.

This helps ensure that you're always aware of what's going on in your industry and of changes that may occur. You can then use these insights to level up your skills and move forward in your industry.

Assist Your Career Development

When it comes to career development, people face hurdles all the time. These hurdles can be because they didn't have the right resources or simply because they didn't know the right person at the right time.

However, all of these concerns can be addressed by networking. Connecting with those who are ahead in their career but in the same field as you allows you to pave your own career path and seek support when needed.

Promote Personal Growth

The truth about networking is that people aren't really comfortable with it. This might be because they're shy, lack communication skills, or just aren't fond of networking. Whatever the case may be, networking requires people to step out of their comfort zone.

But that's not all. Networking allows people to have intellectual discussions and questions about what they already believe. Such discussions allow them to accept the fact they might not be right all the time, and this is what ultimately leads to personal growth.

Contribute to Business Success

Networking is beneficial not only if you're looking to excel in your career as a working professional but also if your ambitions are to have your own thriving business.

Networking allows you to have a broader perspective of the industry, helps you build meaningful connections, and opens up new opportunities. All of this is essential when you start and run a business and can increase your chances of success.

As you can see, networking is essential whether you want to excel in your career or start a business. It helps you grow as a person and as a professional. So, with that in mind, let's look at how you can create your own network.

BUILDING A DIVERSE AND SUPPORTIVE NETWORK

A network that helps you achieve your career goals must be diverse and supportive. Think of these as key elements. What does that mean? It means your network can't just be everyone in your contact lists. It needs to be relevant to what you do and where you plan on going.

A diverse network is one that has professionals from different backgrounds and varying industries that are related to your profession. Having diversity in a network ensures that you're able to explore different perspectives. These perspectives can be about culture, lifestyle, industry changes, wealth, or several other things. But that's not all a diverse network is good for. Diversity gives you access to opportunities in industries you would have never thought you would work in before.

Now, on to supportiveness. Remember when we mentioned that the underlying principle of developing a network is that it's supposed to benefit both you and your connections?

This is what supportiveness is about. When you're building your network, it's okay to have people in it that require your help. However, it's essential that you have individuals who can benefit you, too, because networking is not about giving or taking; it's about sharing. Building such a network is a bit more complicated than handing out business cards.

It's something that will take both time and effort. One of the most important things you need to avoid is being caught up in a networking silo. This happens when you network with those who are in your immediate circle. While it's only natural for us to connect with those we know, doing so within a networking context defeats the entire purpose. We already know what to expect and in which directions conversations will flow. This keeps us from gaining exposure and building meaningful connections.

Now that we've laid the groundwork for building a network let's look at some ways to build one.

Go Outside Your Circle

When it comes to building a diverse network, the first thing you need to do is go outside your circle. Remember, you don't want to be caught up in a networking silo. Those of us who have never connected with anyone outside our immediate circle can find doing so a bit challenging or uncomfortable.

If you want to network with those who are not your go-to contacts, seek to connect with people who have different cultural, religious, or industry-related beliefs than you. To do this, attend events, seminars, or workshops that are outside your usual environment. This could mean that you attend events in different industries or venues and locations you're not familiar with.

When you connect with those who are beyond your immediate circle, you're able to learn about new customs and traditions and develop a new way of thinking. This also gives you access to resources and opportunities to propel your career forward.

Network Online

When you're looking to achieve fulfillment using a dynamic career path, it's likely that you'll switch jobs a few times to find the right fit for you. There's nothing wrong with this; however, it does mean that much of your time will be spent familiarizing yourself with the new role and learning new skills.

Both of these things are essential and might not leave you with enough time to go out, attend events, and connect with others. If you face these circumstances, networking can be done just as effectively online. Discussion boards, forums, online communities, and virtual conferences—the options are endless when it comes to online networking.

Taking part in these online activities and actively contributing to discussions is a great way to connect with individuals all over the world. This not only helps you build meaningful connections but will also allow you to gain a broader understanding. When networking online, remember to show a sense of curiosity and ask open-ended questions.

Connect and Follow-Up

Networking has been around for ages and, for quite a long time, has had a somewhat negative association attached to it. Some people think that networking is about nothing more than connecting with others for their own benefit. Such belief stems from the fact that many people don't really know how to network effectively.

When you're networking, you can't ask people for favors without giving any assistance first, and definitely not without connecting and following up with them. Remember, networking is about having meaningful relationships, and building such relationships takes time. You need to show people that you respect and value their perspectives and beliefs and intend to connect with them.

You also need to follow up with those you connect with. If they've asked you to do something in the past and now you need help, reach out to them. The cornerstone of connection with others is not to be seen as only someone looking to gain but also as someone looking to give.

Collaborate and Share Resources

Another great thing you can do to build a diverse and supportive network is to collaborate and share resources with others. Networking, along with helping and asking for favors, can also be about working together to achieve a common goal. Always look for opportunities where you can partner up with others.

Building a network that emphasizes collaboration is essential. When people within a network collaborate with each other, they can practically demonstrate their knowledge and expertise. It also allows you to ensure that everyone in the network has access to a wealth of different resources and support they can use to excel in their career.

In addition, when people in a network collaborate, they learn from each other in a more productive manner. It also helps them discover innovative ways to work on different projects and tasks.

Believe it or not, building a network that's diverse and provides support is essential to your career fulfillment. It can help you develop a broader perspective about your industry, open up new opportunities, and offer collaboration and support.

With that in mind, let's look at some ways you can make your network efforts more effective.

STRATEGIES FOR EFFECTIVE NETWORKING

Some people believe that networking is only suitable for extroverts or those with charismatic personalities. But that's not really the case. Networking is for everyone, and with the right strategies, anyone can excel at it, even if they're not a smooth talker.

However, some people get frustrated with networking strategies. This happens because they don't know how to use these strategies effectively, and this can lead to self-criticism and doubt. What's even worse is that these things combined can make them feel like an imposter.

This can happen to anyone, so before using these strategies, you need to break free from the mindset that networking is only for extroverts. It requires one to leave one's comfort zone and have conversations with people one doesn't really know, but there's no need for a personality overhaul to network effectively.

By learning and implementing the strategies we're about to share, you, too, can build a network that leads to personal and professional growth and allows you to achieve career fulfillment. These strategies include:

1. **Be prepared ahead of time.** When it comes to networking, the most important thing you must remember is that people you want to connect with are just as busy as you, if not more so. You need to do all the prep work beforehand.

We're not just talking about thinking of what you're going to say. You need to make an appointment with people you're trying to network with and have your resume or business cards handy.

When networking with people at scale, you'll be blown away by the amount of information you have to process. So, it's better to create some sort of organizational system beforehand, too.

2. Present yourself well. All of us have heard that first impressions last, and this holds true for networking more than anything else in the world. So, you need to look at how you present yourself when you're networking.

To improve how you come across, always stand when you're introducing yourself. If you're at a networking event and are wearing a nametag, point to it as you introduce yourself to others.

Don't be afraid to use a firm handshake when greeting others. As you communicate with them and discuss industry-related events and developments, make eye contact.

3. Always have your pitch ready. Another great networking strategy is to always be ready to promote or market yourself on the spot. However, don't come across as too much of a salesperson.

When promoting yourself, you need to be considerate of others' needs. If the person you're communicating with mentions a problem you can solve, by all means, promote what you're capable of. The floor is yours.

If you're at an event where you know people need what you can do, be prepared to market yourself right from the get-go. Practicing how to present your strengths and what you bring to the table in 30 seconds can help you improve your pitch.

4. Ask questions and listen actively. One of the most important things about networking is having conversations that build meaningful relationships. This means those you talk to must feel you're interested in the conversations and that you respect what they say.

The easiest way to add meaning to these conversations is by being an active listener and asking questions. When you ask questions, people think you care about what they're saying, and you want to know more.

It's important to remember that these questions should be open-ended and must facilitate the conversation you're having. This way, you'll not only build meaningful connections but will have an in-depth understanding of the topic being discussed.

5. Value others' opinions and advice. Respect, in networking relationships or any relationship in general, is essential. People are likely to feel respected if they think you value their opinions and advice.

To show that you do, ask them for help on a problem that you're currently facing and follow up with them after implementing their advice. Make sure that those you ask for help from have been through or are going through something similar to your situation.

6. Exchange contact information and follow up. Remember what we discussed about following up? It can also be used as a strategy to network effectively. After the conversation, share your contact information. Always have more than one contact option ready.

Some people might be more comfortable on email than on a call, and others might prefer to text. Cater to their preferences instead of having them cater to yours. This will increase your chances of communicating with that person again.

In addition, it will also make them feel valued. Another thing you can do is make an appointment for a future conversation ahead of time.

7. Constantly grow your network. Your networking efforts shouldn't end once you've reached your objectives. You never know who you'll need to contact.

It's important to make sure that you carry on networking even after you've achieved what you want. Continue to attend events, have conversations, and follow up like before.

Remember, everyone can network, and they should. It allows you to build meaningful relationships with others and can help you grow as a person and a professional.

If there's one thing you should take from this chapter, let it be that networking is about sharing, not taking or giving. In the next chapter, we'll shift our focus to the last part of the FOCUS framework and learn about envisioning your career.

CHAPTER NINE

ENVISION YOUR IDEAL CAREER

 "The mind is the limit. As long as the mind can envision the fact that you can do something, you can do it, as long as you really believe 100 percent."

ARNOLD SCHWARZENEGGER

What you've just read is true; this comes from experience. We've seen so many people think and believe that they can do something extraordinary and then do it. The human mind, when it comes to envisioning how your life should be, is quite powerful.

However, some people confuse visualizing their career with cloudy daydreaming. It's important to know the difference between the two and to know how you can imagine your career in a way that propels you to success. Most people find this to be a challenge, but to be honest, it's something you can do with a little dedicated time and effort.

Envisioning your career is essential when you're working with a non-linear approach. Think back to when you were a child. During those days, when someone would ask you, "What do you want to do when you grow up?" your answer would probably be a top-tier profession like a movie star, an astronaut, or something else along those lines.

Notice that all these professions require an immense level of skills, knowledge, and talent. If someone were to ask a person to pursue such professions during their mid-20s or 30s, they would probably say it's not possible, although the same people would have had no problem believing this as a child.

However, there is something that keeps people from pursuing these ideas and making their dreams come to life. When we're young, we easily believe that we can achieve great success in our professional lives. But this belief deteriorates throughout life, and we find ourselves aiming lower and lower as time passes.

Our beliefs deteriorate when we doubt our abilities and begin to think that we're not competent enough. We experience this doubt for two reasons. One, we don't have clarity about our goal, and two, we don't have an actionable plan. When people experience this at a young age, they lower the target instead of aiming for the higher one. This is what leads to a lack of career fulfillment because deep down inside, these people know they want to do something else entirely.

The first thing to remember is that if you want to envision your ideal career successfully, you need to have a rock-solid belief, clarity, and an actionable plan. In this chapter, we'll look at how you can create smart goals for a dynamic career path. Then, we'll transition to developing a mission statement, creating a roadmap, and using visualization techniques to achieve your career goals.

SMART GOALS

Whenever we think about doing something new, the first thing we need to do is set goals. But do you really know what setting a goal means? Is it just a long-term to-do list, or is it something more than that?

Goal setting is easy if you do it as if you're making a to-do list. But if you set goals like this, the results aren't going to be what you had in mind. All of us have been in a position in life where we've lost track of our goals and have found them to be almost impossible.

In those cases, the problem was not with the goals. It was how the goals were defined. We can lose track of our goals for several reasons. For instance, our goal might be generic, making it difficult to stay dedicated to it. We might not be able to measure our progress, which keeps us from seeing how far we come. Sometimes, we don't have a deadline for achieving that goal.

These things might seem small at first, but they are the difference makers. Setting goals effectively requires you to intend to achieve them within your own capacity.

Also, you can't just copy someone else's goals because this simply won't work. You, your friends, family members, and co-workers all have access to different resources and work at different speeds. Setting goals that will help you achieve career fulfillment requires that you have clarity about what you want to achieve at each stage of your career. We'll talk about this later in the chapter.

Using the SMART framework is a tried-and-tested method that not only helps you create goals that are relevant to you but also increases your chances of achieving them. Smart goals are created based on five criteria.

1. **Specific:** When you're setting your goal, the first thing you need to do is make sure it is specific. This means that you need to keep your goal narrow and simple. It can't be broad or open to interpretation. To make your goal specific, ask yourself:

- What do I want to achieve?
- Where can I achieve this goal?
- Why does this goal matter to me?

Answering these questions will help make your goal less open-ended and more detailed. Let's say that you work in marketing and advertising. In this case, a specific career goal would look like, "I want to lead a marketing and advertising department at an FMCG company so I can ensure that consumers are shown informative ads, allowing them to make better decisions."

2. **Measurable:** The next thing you'll need to do is make sure that your goals are measurable. Many people don't achieve this because they give up if they don't see any immediate results and can't tell if they are making any progress. To prevent this, you need to define metrics for each goal you create. Ask yourself:

- What are my indicators of progress?
- How long will it take me to achieve this goal?
- How will I know I have achieved my goal?

Let's say that you want to learn skills so that you can change your career. A goal that's measurable would look like, "I plan on learning skills associated with my new profession. I'll test each skill I learn to measure my progress. I'll know that I have achieved my goals when my work not only meets but exceeds industry standards."

3. Achievable: Make sure that the goals you set are reasonably achievable. Setting goals in line with what you have and what you're capable of can help make them more achievable. This doesn't mean that you go easy on yourself. Your goals should challenge you. To find a balance with your goals, ask yourself:

- Has someone else done this before?
- Do I have the skills and capabilities needed to achieve this goal?

Working with our previous example, a goal that's achievable could be, "I get off from work at six, and I have around three hours of spare time. If I dedicate those three hours a day to learning, I will acquire new skills within seven to eight months."

4. Relevant: You need to make sure your goals are relevant when you're developing them. Each goal you set should propel you toward achieving career fulfillment. Having relevant goals not only helps you stay on track but also allows you to be more motivated. To make your goal relevant, ask yourself:

- Does this help me achieve career fulfillment?

A goal that is in line with what you really want to do might be, "Learning new skills in about eight months and building credibility will increase my chance of leading the marketing and advertising department."

5. Time-Bound: Last up on the list is time. Some people overlook this aspect, but placing a time limit on your goals is essential. A goal that's not time-specific does not create a sense of urgency, meaning that you won't be motivated to work on it.

To make your goals time-specific, ask yourself when you would like to have achieved that goal. Then, use your answer to set a deadline. If you were to make your goals time-bound, it could look like, "After eight months of education and training, I'll apply for a job and will have changed my career in the following two months."

DESIGNING YOUR CAREER VISION STATEMENT

Now that you know how to create career goals, we'll look at how to create a vision statement for your career. Most people don't give this a second thought and keep it to the extent of writing a resume. However, this statement can be a lot more powerful than that.

When it comes to pursuing a dynamic career path for fulfillment, you'll be shifting from one job to the other every now and then. Oftentimes, this requires skills that you might not have, deadlines you're not comfortable with, and financial constraints. Because of this, people often avoid diversity in their careers or are unsure of how to integrate it.

This is where a career vision statement comes in. During such times, this statement can offer you much-needed clarity and help guide your decision-making. To create such a vision statement, you need to write about how you see yourself in the future but in the PRESENT tense. It is scientifically proven that the mind does not distinguish reality from fiction when we are visualizing (think about biting a lemon, and you will probably feel acidity in your tongue). That is why writing in the present tense is so important; it is a great way to trick your mind into thinking that it has already happened and wire your mind to think in that direction. The reasoning behind creating a career vision statement is to figure out three things:

- Your identity
- Your destination
- Your plan

Before writing a vision statement, you need to engage in self-reflection. To do this, ask yourself about your values, strengths, contributions, and desires. Identifying these things will create a vision statement that's much more valuable than something you just put on a resume. Some great self-reflection questions we've found over the years are:

- What am I good at?
- What's my inner calling?
- What's unique about me?
- Where do I see myself in the future?
- What are my values?
- If there were no obstacles in my way, what would I do?
- If there was one problem I could solve in my industry, what would it be?

Here's an example of what it should look like: "I envision myself as an honest and impactful project leader with global recognition. I aim to build a team where everyone is appreciated, plays towards their strengths, and creates value-added solutions for the end user." Let's look at some key benefits of creating a career vision statement.

- **Offers Direction and Focus:** A career vision statement is a representation of who you are and what you want to be. This means that you can use it to decide whether to pursue an opportunity or not.

- **Keeps You Centered on Your Values:** Your values are a core part of your vision statement. This means when you use a vision statement to make decisions, they are automatically in line with what you believe is right.
- **Shapes Your Definition of Success:** The definition of success some people have is based on others' perspectives. Creating a vision statement helps you acknowledge what you value and allows you to have your own definition of success.
- **Evolves as You Progress:** A vision statement is not something that's concrete. You can update it as you make progress, meaning that it will provide you with directional clarity throughout your career.

CREATING A CAREER ROADMAP

Now that you know how to create a vision statement, let's take the next step and learn to build a career map. This is a tool you can use to plan the steps needed to achieve a professional goal. It also helps you identify opportunities to explore and allows you to put your priorities in order.

When people hear that a career map can be used to plan your entire career, they think that making one will be quite a challenge, but that's not the case. In fact, you can create a career map for yourself by following a series of simple steps. The best part is that we've already covered what you need to do for most of the steps in previous chapters.

Set Goals

The first thing you must do to build a personal career map is to set goals simply because there's no point in having a map if you don't know where you're going. Remember, the goals you set need to be SMART, as we discussed earlier in the chapter.

However, before setting your goals, indulge in some self-reflection. Figure out what you're good at and where there's room for improvement. Also, take the time to identify your passion and core values, as this will help you make career choices that align with who you really are.

You can refer back to Chapter 2 for a quick refresher on exploring your inner landscape if you're having a hard time with self-reflection.

Identify Skill Gaps

Once you've determined your goals, take the time to identify the skills you'll need to achieve those goals. Focus on both soft and technical skills. You can refer to Chapter 6 to review how to do that.

Sometimes, people compromise their goals because they don't have the skills needed to achieve them. However, learning and acquiring skills is lifelong, and you need to have a growth mindset. You can refer to Chapter 7 if you want to review that. Remember, there are different methods, like workshops and courses, you can pursue to learn skills.

Identify Networking Opportunities

The next thing you need to do when creating a career map is determine how you're going to network with others to achieve your goals. Know that networking is essential regardless of where you are in your career, as it helps you gain a broader perspective and allows you to have access to more opportunities.

With networking, always remember that the idea is not to give or take but to share. Before you can ask someone for a favor, you need to help them out. The options for networking are endless. You can connect and build relationships with others at events, conferences, and online forums. Refer to the previous chapter if you need a quick refresher.

Create Milestones

Once you've identified your goals, skill gaps, and networking opportunities, you're ready to put your career map to use. However, before you do, remember to break down your long-term goals into smaller and more manageable objectives and set milestones.

If one of your goals is to change careers and shift to a different industry, break this down into smaller objectives. In this case, smaller objectives or milestones might include familiarizing yourself with the industry and learning the required skills. You can look at Chapter 7 to review how to navigate industry changes.

Monitor and Revise

Lastly, you need to monitor and revise your career maps as you make progress. The underlying principle of pursuing a dynamic career approach is to explore different options until you find the one that is right for you. As you shift from one job role or industry to another, remember to reassess your goals and make necessary changes to your career map.

USE VISUALIZATION TO REACH YOUR CAREER GOALS

The last thing you must do to realize your ideal career is use visualization. Visualization is the act of feeling, seeing, and embodying a future outcome.

This outcome can be you changing your career or getting that promotion with the corner office you've been working so hard for. Visualizing a desired outcome in your mind with as much detail as possible can help you transform it into a reality. When you visualize something in such detail, your brain interprets it as reality.

You trick your brain into thinking that the desired outcome has already happened. This way, you can take action that aligns with that perceived reality. Visualization allows you to see yourself achieving a desired result before it actually happens.

You can use this mental image and work backward, creating small steps that help you turn that image into a reality. Here are some of the most effective visualization techniques.

- **Mental Rehearsals:** This practice requires you to imagine completing all the tasks required to achieve your goals.
- **Affirmations:** This technique requires you to describe your goals as if you've already achieved them. The key here is to eliminate the "What if" thoughts.

- **Vision Boards:** This technique requires you to lay out your vision or roadmap of goals on a board and add pictures of what you want to achieve to the board.
- **Meditation:** There are lots of ways to meditate, but the underlying aim is to detach yourself from the stress of future outcomes and focus on the present moment.
- **Sensory Experiences:** Visualize achieving your goals down to the smallest detail possible and create a complete sensory experience. If you see yourself celebrating with champagne, imagine how it tastes.

Remember that conceiving your ideal career is necessary for achieving fulfillment. It allows you to have much-needed directional clarity and help you make better career choices. When envisioning your ideal career, set SMART goals and use them alongside self-reflection to create a career vision statement.

You also need to make a career map, as it allows you to plan the steps you need to take to achieve your goals. Lastly, visualize achieving your goals and work backward from that mental image by creating small steps that will help you achieve fulfillment.

Now that you know how to think about and envision your ideal career, we'll take all of this planning and learn to put it into action.

CHAPTER TEN

CALL TO ACTION

 "Dream big, start small, but most of all, start."

SIMON SINEK

As we near the end of this book, remember that we've covered quite a lot of great content that will help you achieve fulfillment in your professional life. We covered everything from understanding the dynamic career path to exploring who you are and bouncing back from failure to networking.

However, none of that will do you any good unless you act on it. To be honest, how fast you move and make progress doesn't really matter. What does matter is that you move forward and keep doing so despite the challenges life throws your way and the failures you face.

Understanding what keeps people from acting on their plans will help you limit the impact of such things on your life and will allow you to move forward. That's exactly what we're going to talk about in this last chapter. We'll discuss how you can go from thinking and planning to doing, and you'll learn about things that can help you take action.

FROM THINKING AND PLANNING TO DOING

There are five birds sitting on a branch, and four of them plan to fly off. How many are left? If you answered one, we've got news for you. The correct answer is five because there's a difference between planning and doing. That difference is what we're going to talk about.

There is nothing wrong with thinking or planning about what you're going to do as long as you do it. Why don't people act? This can vary from person to person. Common excuses for not acting can include:

- Fear
- Lack of time
- No motivation
- Lack of energy

What we found is that all these things prevail because people are uncertain of what the results of their actions would be. They fear that acting might lead to failure, which is why they don't make the time for it. Given this, they are not motivated and lack the energy to take action.

One way to get over this is to acknowledge that the only thing that's certain is that nothing will happen if you don't act. Here are some of the easiest and most effective things you can do to take action.

Know That Conditions Will Never Be Perfect

Most people don't take action because they think the time is not right. The time will never be right. There will almost always be something that could be different or better. However, what could be different for the better can also be different for the worse. The best time to take action was yesterday; the second-best time to act is today, and there might not be a third.

Stop Procrastinating

All of us know that procrastination is when we think about doing something or know that we should do something, and we promise ourselves we'll do it later but never get to it. Why does this happen? If we hold off on something for too long, we lose the motivation to act, and that task keeps dropping down our priority list step-by-step until it's not even there. The easiest way to stop procrastination is to just get up and take action.

Don't Overthink

Overthinking is much more serious and prevalent than people realize. Excessive overthinking can lead to an analysis-paralysis condition where you keep thinking and don't act—the time is not right, the conditions are not right, so many things could go wrong. The truth about thinking too much is that it will create problems that never existed in the first place, and the only solution is to act.

Build Momentum

One of the best things you can do to go from being a thinker to a doer is to build momentum. Taking action at the start might be a bit challenging, but once you've done that, continue to do it. You don't have everything at once. Instead, dedicate a small amount of time to acting towards each of your goals every day, as it can help you build the confidence and momentum needed to succeed.

Act Despite Fear

Fear is one of the most common things that keeps people from acting because they are too concerned about whether they will reach their desired outcome. However, as we discussed in a previous chapter, such fears are not definitive if you see them as a learning opportunity. Fear can also come from a lack of confidence or capability. The only way to overcome fear is to act in spite of it and use the experience to learn and improve.

Focus on the Now

Live in and focus on the present moment. People spend too much time thinking about how things could be if they had acted a certain way in the past or do so in the future. It's easy to get caught up in these thoughts, and it's equally important to remember that you don't have control over the past or future, so instead of thinking about them, it's better to act now.

Eliminate Distractions

Lastly, another common reason that keeps people from taking action is distractions. We give in to distractions because they give us immediate gratification. To keep yourself from doing this, don't just identify and eliminate the distractions. Focus on what triggers you to give in to those distractions and eliminate those triggers, too.

And with that, we've reached the end of this book. Up next, we'll quickly go over what we've learned, but if there's one thing you should take from this chapter, let it be that "done is better than perfect".

CONCLUSION

 "One average idea put into action is far more valuable than 20 genius ideas that are being saved."

CHRIS SHILLING

First of all, we would like to congratulate you on completing this book. We covered some great content on how to implement a dynamic career path and achieve fulfillment in your professional life.

We started off our journey by learning that having the non-linear advantage means being willing and able to explore multiple career opportunities. However, before implementing a dynamic approach to career growth and fulfillment, you need to know that the modern career landscape is evolving.

Remember that these changes are driven by social, economic, and technological factors. It's essential that you stay updated with these changes. Doing so will allow you to identify and acquire skills that can help you leverage the changes and excel. However, to find opportunities resulting in fulfillment, you need to know where fulfillment comes from.

Fulfillment is the result or experience you get when your profession aligns with who you really are. To find such opportunities, you first need to explore your inner self by identifying your passion, strengths, and true calling. This is often easier said than done, and to do this, you should know the difference between passion and hobbies.

You can also take the different strength tests we've mentioned in the book and identify what you're good at. Think about what makes you happy and brings you joy. Above all, remember to truly explore your inner self in a continuous journey of self-discovery.

When you have identified your passion, strengths, and true calling, use these insights to develop your personal brand. Personal branding is essential, as it helps you create your digital footprint and enables professional growth. When creating a personal brand, remember that it's about presenting your unique story in a meaningful way.

Things like your skills, qualifications, achievements, core beliefs, and values should be a part of your personal brand. In addition, you should also use social media, blogging, and speaking at industry events to grow your personal brand and build competence within your niche.

As you work towards implementing a non-linear career path, you will encounter failures. This can be anything from challenges to beat or setbacks that could hold you back. It's important for you to use all of them as stepping stones on your road to fulfillment and success.

To do this, you must first conquer the fear of failure or learn to act despite it. The fear of failure originates from your thinking that fear is a result that's definitive. To overcome it, you must realize that fear is only definitive if you refuse to take action once you have failed.

If you use your failures as experiences to learn more, they will become just part of the process. Fear can also come from the uncertainties of life. They lead to fear because, during those times, we don't really know how to act. However, this is something you can address by identifying your guiding light.

This guiding light can be your beliefs, values, or goals. When faced with uncertainty, ask yourself if what you plan to do aligns with these things, and use the answers to pave the way. Whenever you face fear or self-doubt, remember to question it, think back to times you've overcome it before, and ask for feedback.

In addition, you should also learn to avoid negative self-talk by replacing the "I can't" with "I can." We also talked about the fact that to achieve career fulfillment, you need to embody the entrepreneurial spirit. This means that you need to think like an entrepreneur and familiarize yourself with that mindset.

You should also identify key characteristics and traits that make entrepreneurs different and develop them. To achieve success in finding career fulfillment, you need to take risks; however, this doesn't mean that you put a blindfold on and walk into the abyss.

You need to take risks like an entrepreneur by weighing the pros and cons associated with each risk. We also mentioned how you can start your business. To do this like an entrepreneur, you need to identify trends, fill market gaps, and solve the problems your target audience faces.

Throughout the book, we've talked about the importance of becoming a lifelong learner. Following a dynamic career path requires you to change job roles and industries until you find an opportunity that's truly right for you. To do all this, you must analyze your skills tool kit.

This will help you determine what you lack. You can then use these insights and fill in the skills using different learning resources. Common examples of such resources may include online courses, books, workshops, training sessions, and so on. Remember that lifelong learning is essential and beneficial to both your personal and professional growth.

Developing the habit of becoming a learner will also help you adapt to the changing world around you. When you pursue a dynamic career path, you will have to shift to different industries and navigate the changes that lie within these industries. Knowing how to learn will help you be more adaptable to change and will increase your chances of success.

Networking will also help you with your pursuit of career fulfillment. It allows you to build meaningful relationships with those in your industry and with those connected to your industry. However, the idea of networking is not to give or take but to share.

Visualize your success, as it can help you turn that mental image into a reality. And finally, remember that all this knowledge will only do you good if you act on it, so you need to take action.

Begin your journey to a dynamic career now. Stop waiting, take charge of your destiny, transform your professional life, and achieve fulfillment today!

If you've found this book helpful, leave a review and recommend it to someone who's also struggling with their career.

If you have any questions, send us an email to ines@arescoaching.com and we will personally reply to you!

And remember to follow our certified coach on Instagram for daily tips on mindset work, entrepreneurship and taking action on your goals. Follow on Instagram under the username: @ares.energycoaching

Good luck!

REFERENCES

Elad, Barry. "Career Change Statistics By Age, Gender, Education, Reasons and Benefits." *Enterprise Apps Today* (blog), June 26, 2023. https://www.enterpriseapp stoday.com/stats/career-change-statistics.html.

Gyfted. "Work Strengths Assessment - Free Work Strengths Test," n.d. https://www.gyfted.me/quiz-landing/work-strengths.

Hobbs, Leslie. "Gianluca Iaccarino: Don't Be Afraid of the Non-Linear Career Path | Stanford University School of Engineering." Stanford Engineering. Stanford University, March 2, 2022. https://engineering.stanford.edu/magazine/gianluca-iaccarino-dont-be-afraid-non-linear-career-path.

Inc, Gallup. "CliftonStrengths." Gallup.com, n.d. https://www.gallup.com/clifton strengths/en/252137/home.aspx.

UNICEF. "Young People Unable to Access Skills Needed for Today's Job Market, New Report Says," December 10, 2021. https://www.unicef.org/press-releases/young-people-unable-access-skills-needed-todays-job-market-new-report-says.

VIA Institute. "VIA Character Strengths Survey & Character Reports | VIA Institute," n.d. https://www.viacharacter.org/.

Manufactured by Amazon.ca
Bolton, ON

41199056R00087